D1403395

# BOYS IN THE HOODS

## ONE MAN'S JOURNEY FROM HATRED TO LOVE

### AN AUTOBIOGRAPHICAL EXPOSÉ OF RACIAL HATRED, RACISM, AND REDEMPTION

## JOHNNY LEE CLARY

**PNEUMA LIFE**

PUBLISHING

# Boys in the Hoods

**Johnny Lee Clary**

Unless otherwise noted, Scripture quotations are taken from the New International Version. Copyright 1973, 1978, 1984, International Bible Society. Scripture quotations marked KJV are from the King James Version of the Bible.

Printed in the United States of America.
ISBN: 1-56229-448-2

# Contents

Acknowledgement
Dedication
Foreword
Preface
Introduction

# Acknowledgements

Many thanks to these fine people who helped me complete this book as well as those who have supported this ministry:

David Vivas who has been a tremendous help to this ministry

Pastors Juan and Kathy Juarez

Derwin Stewart

Gary and Carolyn Ellison

Yvonne Lamb

Debra Petrosky

ICFM and Azusa Fellowship for ordaining me

Jeff Fenholt

Paul and Jan Crouch

Laura Massey of the Trinity Broadcasing Network

Billy Joe and Sharon Daughtery

Carlton Pearson

Uncle Wade Watts

Tia Watts

Rev. Paul Sinclair

Andy Bassel

Rosie Stammon

Penilopee Summerlin

Amel McLaughlin

Oprah Winfrey

Geraldo Rivera

Sally Jesse Raphael

Montel Williams

Morton Downey, Jr.

Phil Donahue

Del and Cindy Way

Pat Robertson of the 700 Club

Rev. Bill Means

Leonard Kimble

Jackie Mason

Bishop George McKinney

And all the pastors who have supported my ministy by allowing me to minister at their churches.

# Dedication

This book is dedicated to the memory of my grandmother, Mrs. Mamie (Nan-Nan) Carter (1908-1995), without whose prayers I would not have changed and become the person I am today.

# Foreword

Growing up as a young black man, I heard horror stories about the mistreatment of many of my ancestors suffered at the hands of the Ku Klux Klan. I would never have dreamed that one day a former Imperial Wizard of the KKK would be a friend and a member of my church.

One day in 1988, I sat glued to my television, watching the Morton Downey talk show. The guest that day was the current Heartland Director of the White Aryan Resistance. He would soon become a National Leader as Imperial Wizard of the Ku Klux Klan in Oklahoma. This bitter racist's inflammatory remarks ignited a back-fire within my spirit. It was a flame of resistance.

For 23 years, I had endeavored to quench the fire of racism with my own fervor for racial unity. My church and ministry, based in the affluent area of a southern city, had been foremost in pursuing this purpose. I had watched as blacks and whites worshiped and fellowshiped together. I saw understanding and respect for differences unity a congregation. A body of believers became one voice as they praised God. We were one—heart and mind.

This particular day however, a man was telling millions it could not be done. There could be no harmony with a race he felt was inferior in every way.

Without hesitation I made one of the most important calls of my life. I called on the one who had summoned me to a higher purpose. I had no idea I would one day come face to face with a renewed, redeemed Johnny Lee Clary. In 1992, he stood before me as a member of my congregation. I have watched, in amazement, Johnny Lee tell his sometimes terrifying but always touching testimony.

You will discover within these pages the story of his dynamic deliverance from the David Duke theology. His journey into the divine truth of the Word of God will astound you. As he walks from the base of a burning cross to the foot of the blood stained cross of Calvary, you will experience his transformation.

It is a humble honor to recommend the testimony of this Elder of our own Azusa Interdenominational Fellowship of Churches and Ministries. In the same year Nelson Mandela became President of a racially ravaged nation, a former Imperial Wizard of the Ku Klux Klan began to preach the Gospel of Jesus Christ to another nation at risk. Truly times are changing.

Prepare to be first outraged then radically changed by the challenging testimony of Johnny Lee Clary.

Carlton D. Pearson

# **Preface**

One day when I was five years old, I was sitting in a car with my father in front of a grocery store in Del City, Oklahoma, a small town outside of Oklahoma City. The year was 1964, and it was the first time in my life that I had seen a black person.

As the black man walked out of the store, I sat amazed and shocked. Turning to my father, I exclaimed, "Look, Daddy, a chocolate covered man!"

My father looked at me and replied, "Son, that is not a chocolate covered man. That's a 'nigger.' Say 'nigger,' son; say 'nigger.'"

Innocent and unsuspecting, I blared out the window of the car, "Nigger, nigger, nigger!"

My dad laughed hilariously, jabbing his cigar into his mouth and blowing a puff of smoke in the air.

That incident marked the day when the first seed of racism was planted in my heart.

Today as I reflect on those early years, I wonder if my father would have instructed me to utter that racial epithet had he known that by planting that seed of hatred and bigotry in my life I would one day grow up to join the Ku Klux Klan. I spent 17 years in the Klan organization as a bodyguard for the notorious David Duke and as the right-hand man to the arch white supremacist, Tom Metzger, who by all accounts is one of the most violent men to ever preach racial hatred. Eventually, I became an imperial wizard, rising to the top of the Klan as one of the most nefarious Klan leaders in the nation.

Racism is not a disease or mental disorder that one inherits at birth. Racism is an ideology and mind-set that is taught — a perspective that is conveyed and then developed as a result of the racist behavior and attitudes of those with whom we associate.

A child does not come into this world hating and putting down other people because of the color of their skin. One can only learn to hate by those who wield influence over his or her life, such as a parent, a grandparent, an older brother or sister, an aunt or an uncle, or a teacher or friends at school. If a child ends up hating someone else or seeing a difference in someone solely based on race — and thinks himself to be superior or inferior because of that difference — it is because of what someone has taught that child. Hatred is a learned response. Simply put, racism is an acquired attitude.

Racial hatred and bigotry in America are time bombs waiting to explode in the hearts of men. These poisons have destroyed the lives of many people, and, as Americans, we must learn to overcome them if we are to live in peace.

This book relates my personal experiences of promoting racial prejudice. I am firmly convinced that the only way to overcome racial hatred and bigotry is through educating people about race and politics. Leaving behind a lifetime of intolerance is difficult but not impossible. It may not occur all at once, but it can happen.

My purpose in writing this book is to provide a measure of education, information, and awareness about the ideology of racism and one of its oldest and greatest proponents, the Ku Klux Klan. More importantly, I trust and pray that I can give hope to the hundreds of thousands of men and women who have been either the victims or perpetrators of racial hatred. My desire is to let these people know there is purpose for their lives as well as their pain. No matter how greatly overcome one is by hate, bigotry, and racism, I am here to tell you a light shines at the end of the tunnel of despair.

If someone hates another it is because, on the inside, they really hate themselves. As a result of their inability to discover a true love of God and self, they begin to act out their hatred for self toward other people. Maybe these people have suffered; maybe they have come from impoverished backgrounds (the so-called wrong side of the tracks); maybe they have been hurt; maybe they come from a dysfunctional family. Whatever the case may be, they are not satisfied with themselves and think they will feel better about themselves by putting down other people.

The typical psychological profile of the average klansman reveals a physically grown-up male who has yet to resolve his inner conflict with an early adulthood or childhood failure to receive unconditional love. This inevitably results in a negative self-perception. These klansmen are children in men's bodies, children without the resolve to love themselves. Therefore, instead of being able to "love thy neighbor as thyself," klansmen hate their neighbor in the same manner and degree in which they hate themselves. Klansmen are boys without the character and fortitude to assume responsibility for their actions or for the destiny of their lives. They are immature, hiding their childish but destructive behavior behind white-hooded sheets: "boys in the hoods."

These people, along with others who have yet to come to a healthy love for self, must be told that there is hope for them too. If you doubt that a vindictive, intolerant person can change, my story proves that no one is beyond hope.

# Introduction

Several exposes and documentaries have been conducted on the origin, operations, and present status of the Ku Klux Klan. The intent of this book, however, is not specifically to present information about the history of the Klan and how the organization presently carries out its agenda. The purpose of *Boys in the Hoods* is to address the fears, anxieties, and insecurities that motivate and promote such racist attitudes.

The Ku Klux Klan, in the most basic political and social assessment, is generally referred to as an extremist right-wing, pro-white supremacist organization. We contend that the racially indifferent attitudes and behaviors of average Americans instigate and give purpose to violent, extremist organizations such as the Klan. Therefore, in his Klan expose and autobiography, former KKK imperial wizard Johnny Lee Clary, endeavors to explore, expose, and explain the commonly accepted attitudes and social perceptions that make otherwise average American citizens susceptible to Klan exploitation and other extreme elements of white supremacist beliefs and activities.

Our objective also is to reveal and explain the foundational elements for extreme racist philosophies and behaviors. Additionally, we will discuss the American church's unwillingness, reluctance, neglect, and silence when it comes to addressing issues of race.

Ironically, racism in America has gained its validation, legitimization, accreditation, societal acceptance, and moral endorsement from the church and other pro-religious institutions. Men of evil intent and corrupt morality have used the Bible to promote a fallacious belief in the superiority of the so-called white race and the inferiority of people of color. This book concludes with realistic, biblically-based solutions to the problem of racism, especially the subtle but destructive type of racism that has been tolerated — and in many instances condoned and practiced — by certain elements of the church and the Christian community of America.

We hope that the story of Johnny Lee Clary's turbulent past of racism, hatred, and bigotry will be a motivating force to change the racist attitudes of those who read this book.

Gary B. Ellison, Project Editor
Boys in the Hoods

# Chapter One

# Tilling the Soil

From the time of its inception, the Ku Klux Klan has gone through a number of successive eras marked by expansion and decline.

The Klan began in the South shortly after the Civil War as a white supremacist and protectionist reaction to the political and governmental reconstruction that was taking place. The Klan's reaction was specifically in response to freed slaves asserting their rights and in fear of supposed black renegades who were suspected of seeking revenge on their former slaves owners and their families.

The Ku Klux Klan (from the Greek word *kuklos*, meaning circle or wheel) was founded by a group of young ex-confederate soldiers in Pulaski, Tennessee, in 1865 at the end of the Civil War. The KKK hunted down any blacks suspected of harassing and challenging whites, which was the basis of the Klan's initial existence. Within three years, Klan branches sprouted in most southern states, and membership eventually grew to more than half a million.

It was the Klan's belief that Christianity meant whites were supreme and blacks were inferior, sub-human beings. This twisted and erroneous belief also gave validity and sanctions to the immoral institution of the European slave trade. After the Civil War, this belief became the basis for a barrage of violence carried out against blacks, including arson, beatings, rapes, terrorism, and murders.

In response to the uninhibited and unrestrained violence, Congress enacted a law in 1871 outlawing the KKK for "conspiring to deprive people of their civil rights." By the mid-1870s, the Klan was discredited across much of the South, and memberships begin to drop drastically. However, the ideology of white supremacy adamantly reinforced by the KKK had been  firmly rooted in the South.

As a result of the South's common adherence to racism, many of the laws outlawing the conduct of the KKK eventually were overturned. Over the next 10 years, the U.S. Supreme Court also began to whittle away persistently at many of the federal laws enacted to curb Klan violence. The Klan was revived.

The end of the 19th century marked a time when millions of new immigrant settlers came to America, arousing the fears of many whites. This, along with D.W. Griffith's motion picture *The Birth of a Nation* in 1915, which gave an idealistic, heroic portrayal of the KKK, sparked a new and explosive growth in Klan membership. By the early 1920s, the Ku Klux Klan claimed, and accurately so, as many as four million members nationwide.

In its attempt to increase and multiply its membership the Klan, through the print media and public intimidation of blacks and minorities, manipulated and exploited white America's fear of crime, the emergence of big urban cities, and the influx of foreigners. Such propaganda resulted in many white Americans believing that they needed to rely on organizations that were more concerned about their welfare than the government seemed to be. Hence the popularity of the Klan grew even more.

The Ku Klux Klan further increased its credibility and respectability by aligning itself with Protestant clergy, one of the many church organizations and religious institutions that gave an erroneous biblical and religious sanction to the European slave trade. This alliance precipitated many local businessman and civic leaders openly becoming members of the Klan without any social reservations or ramifications.

Warren G. Harding, the 29th President of the United States, became an honorary member of the Ku Klux Klan at a swearing in ceremony in the White House. Hugo Black, as a young lawyer and a recognized Klan member, became a U.S. Senator. Black went on to serve as a Supreme Court Justice for some 34 years until 1971.

On August 8, 1925, the popularity of the Klan reached its height as 30,000 Klan members, hooded and carrying American and confederate flags, marched through the streets of the nation's capital in conspicuous display of white supremacy and defiance against the elected and official powers of the day.

This popularity did not endure for too long, however. Later that year, the grand dragon of the Indiana branch of the Ku Klux Klan was implicated, indicted, convicted, and sentenced to life in prison for the rape and murder of a young white woman. Exiled by the Klan, the former grand dragon began to retaliate by exposing corruption within the organization. This scandal resulted in a great decline in Klan membership, from four million to under two million by 1930.

In an attempt to regain membership and popularity, the Klan began to align itself with other right-wing, white supremacist organizations such as the Nazi-styled German American Bund. When the United States declared war against Fascism in 1941, however, white supremacist extremism became unpopular and un-American, and an actual threat to U.S. national security. This national intolerance of the Klan's actions marked the beginning of the KKK's second descent toward obscurity. In 1944, the Klan became bankrupt after the government ruled that it was delinquent in paying $700,000 in back taxes.

After the troublesome and what appeared to be devastating events of the 1940s, it appeared that the Ku Klux Klan organization was nearly dead. But

America's social and political climate during post World War II dictated something else: a renewed zeal in Klan activity and Klan affinity. After the war, many soldiers returned home to the South to find it as poverty stricken, prejudiced, and racist as ever. When the federal government, set on dismantling segregation, began to enforce civil rights laws, many whites stood defiantly against the will of the civil rights movement of the 1950s and 1960s. The South's opposition to desegregation sparked the revival of many local chapters of the Ku Klux Klan.

The U.S. Supreme Court decision of May 17, 1954, in the case of *Brown vs. The Board of Education*, ruled that racial segregation in public schools was unconstitutional and a violation of students' civil rights. Nevertheless, the enforcement of the ruling was met with much opposition. Three years later in December 1957, after the declaration of the new law against racial segregation in public schools, President Dwight D. Eisenhower had to deploy 1,000 federal troops to Little Rock, Arkansas to protect nine new black students from a vicious and angry mob of whites who violently protested the black integration of the southern white-only schools.

Klan members reacted in their usual fashion by inciting another terrorist crusade against blacks living in the South. In Montgomery, Alabama, Klan members bombed several homes and churches of black citizens.

The Klan found itself most popular and active during the time of the civil rights era, where its members vehemently opposed racial integration. Since that time the Klan has gone through a number of changes and transitions. From hooded "red necks," to politicians and governmental and judicial figures, to white youth with shaved heads who refer to themselves as skinheads and soldiers of the White Aryan Resistance (WAR).

The following story depicts my experiences as a young man whose troubled life, combined with the influence of a racist father, caused me to be susceptible to the manipulation and exploitation of one of America's most feared — and at one time most respected — hate-motivated, white supremacist organizations, the Ku Klux Klan. The soil was fertile for the planting of seeds of hate.

# Chapter Two

# A Story to Tell

I am told that I was my father's love child, conceived in a weekend of calculated passion to save a rocky marriage. By the time I was born on June 18, 1959 in Martinez, California, William Walter Clary and Billie Jean Tyler Clary had been married at least seven-and-a-half years and had two other children — seven-year-old Larry Allen and six-year-old Sandra Sue. Another boy, Terry Don, would be born three-and a-half years after my birth, but for years I was the one on whom my father doted.

When I was six months old, my family moved to Oklahoma. It was a return to familiar soil for my parents, who had met in Oklahoma City and later moved to California in 1950.

The first 11 years of my topsy-turvy childhood were spent on Shalimar Drive in Del City, Oklahoma, a suburb of Oklahoma City. It was a small town back in the 1960s where everybody knew everybody and everybody knew everybody else's business.

My father, an industrious paint contractor, worked for 11 years for Harkins Brothers Paint Corporation, eventually becoming a foreman. His job took him out of town quite a bit, but he always provided for his family.

My father looked, sounded, dressed, and acted like a southern Archie Bunker. Except for his southern accent and muscular boxer arms, you could say that in facial resemblance and bigoted attitudes, he was Archie Bunker. And in absolute Archie Bunker spirit, I always heard him spewing racial epithets around the house. Ironically, I loved and admired everything about my father.

My attitude toward my mother, however, was quite different. She definitely was not June Cleaver or even Edith Bunker for that matter. Many times I came home from school and found her sitting in her armchair, putting on makeup and drinking a beer, preparing to go out to a bar.

A pretty woman with long dark hair and the good looks of Loretta Young, my mother was an ex-country and western singer — and an alcoholic. Her life with my father was full of strife. I believe she drank to forget. What she was trying to forget, I never knew. She was rarely at home and spent a lot of her time in bars. I knew that my mother often cheated on my father, which led to many fights between the two of them in our home.

I remember a song called "Skip a Rope," which was made popular in the 1960s by country and western singer Henson Cargill. He sang, "Daddy hates Mommy; Mommy hates Dad. Last night you should have heard the fight they had. Gave little sister another bad dream and woke us all up with a terrible scream. Skip a rope." I remember hearing this on the radio and thinking he must know my mother and my father because this song sounds just like my family.

I watched my father and mother yelling and screaming at each other. Sometimes those boisterous arguments spilled into the yard. Many times the fights got so bad the neighbors called the police. The cops came to the house at all hours of the night. I often wondered why my father and mother continued to live together.

My mother frequently ran off with other men. On those nights when my father came home and discovered her gone, he would jump in his car and search honkytonks and bars until he found her. Finding her in the arms of some man, he often beat the guy senseless, almost killing him; then he beat my mother and dragged her home. That would be the beginning of another long battle between them. They yelled and screamed at each other, but my father always patched things up. In some odd kind of way, my father must have truly loved my mother.

My life as a child bounced up and down like a seesaw. Unfortunately, most of it was on the down side. My older brother and sister were jealous because my father showed me lots of attention and open favoritism. My father took me on fishing trips and whenever I wanted something, if I asked my father, I almost always got it. This was not the same for Larry and Sandy. My father spent a lot of time with me, causing my older brother and sister to resent me.

Because he was so much younger than us, my little brother was not always aware of my father's favoritism. Terry Don also spent a lot of time with my grandparents who adored him and took him to their home on weekends. As a result, he avoided many of the fights and other traumatic things that happened within our family.

My mother and father drank constantly, which caused many of their problems. I remember my father coming home and dancing in the kitchen and teaching songs to me like "Ak a back a soda cracka, ak a back a boo; if your mother chews tobacco, she's a dirty Jew." At the time I didn't even know what a Jew was. I just knew that Daddy said "dirty Jew," and by using that term I just assumed that all Jews were dirty.

My father did not use words such as black, Negro, or colored to identify people of African-American ethnicity; he always said the word "nigger" and taught me to do the same.

Because my father used the word "nigger" in identifying and describing African Americans, I again —

as in the case of the derogatory Jewish description — presupposed that the word nigger was the appropriate term to use when referring to all people perceived to be black. I soon learned differently but continued to call blacks "niggers" because it pleased my father.

On Saturday nights my father and mother normally went out drinking. They never went to church, but they were firm believers in sending their children to Sunday school. Every Sunday morning the four of us were put on the Sunday school bus while my parents stayed in bed trying to sleep off their hangovers. Sending us to Sunday school seemed to be a good way to get us out of the house.

Although he always kept two rosaries hanging in the front room and claimed to be a Catholic, my father was not a religious man. My mother maintained that she was a Christian, but it was hard to believe by the way she and my dad drank, cursed, and smoked. Neither of them ever went to church, so God was not first in their lives nor the head of our home.

One day on the Sunday school bus, I looked out the window and saw a little black boy on a bicycle at a gas station where the bus had stopped to get fuel. I rolled down the window and hollered at him. "Hey, nigger!" I yelled and then went back to my seat.

The Sunday school teacher who was on the bus asked, "Johnny Lee, what did you say?" I told her, and she said, "Ah, did you?"

The teacher then began to sing the song: "Jesus loves the little children, all the children of the world. Red and yellow, black and white, we are precious in His sight. Jesus loves the little children of the world."

I couldn't wait to get home and tell my daddy what I had learned from the Sunday school teacher. Needless to say, I found myself going to another church not long after that.

I remember another incident that occurred when our family was eating in a restaurant. As a group of black men walked through the door, my father started yelling from behind his menu, "Nigger, nigger, nigger!" He kept saying that word as the black men looked around the restaurant to see from whom and where the insulting remarks were coming. I sat there and laughed. At the time, the incident seemed funny.

When my daddy took me fishing, I considered that our quality time together. Our fishing expeditions were some of the most special times that I shared with my daddy.

My father was my hero. He was the toughest man in the neighborhood. I used to always brag that Daddy, a former golden gloves boxer with 73 knockouts, could beat up any of the other dads in the neighborhood.

I idolized and practically worshiped my father and wanted to be just like him. When he spewed racial slurs I repeated them with the same vigor and passion that he did. I was on my way to becoming a bigoted racist.

# Chapter Three

# "There Goes the Neighborhood!"

The first time a black family moved into our neighborhood, they bought a house on Del Rancho Street, about two blocks from Shalimar Drive where we lived.

My father was so angry at hearing the news he began screaming and hollering. "I can't believe that a bunch of niggers have moved just two blocks away! Can you believe it?"

This was the only time that I could recall my neighborhood ever being united. Before the black family moved into the neighborhood, the neighbors were always fighting with each other. As would be expected, no one really liked my dad, and of course my dad didn't like anyone either. But one thing was for sure, no one wanted blacks living so close.

One day while I was playing on Del Rancho Street, I saw some of the white neighborhood children with some of the youngsters from the black family.

A white girl grabbed a ball and hit one of the black girls with it, yelling, "You fat nigger!"

"Don't call us names," the little black girl pleaded.

I laughed hilariously at the little black girl and told the little white girl she shouldn't be playing with black kids anyway.

I began to make up little songs. These were not nice songs, but they made me feel good. I taunted and yelled, "Nigger, nigger, nigger," at them, and then I sang derogatory songs. Feeling superior, I put down these children, and they could do nothing to stop me. Something inside me said they were inferior to me.

I thought black people stunk, therefore, I didn't even want to touch them. If a person was black, I didn't want to associate with them in any way whatsoever. As a child I was already well programmed in the art of bigotry and racial hatred.

Before long, the government built Hamilton Courts, a housing complex just a few blocks from our home. Because of it more black families began to move into the area. My father responded, "Well, that's it. There goes the neighborhood!"

Before blacks moved into the neighborhood, I left my bicycle out in the yard at night. But my dad warned me, "From now on, Johnny Lee, you'll have to take your bicycle and put it in the garage at night; otherwise you'll get up in the morning and your bike will be gone. Those niggers are going to steal it."

We used to go to sleep at night with our door unlocked, but after the black families moved in, my father said, "We're going to have to start locking the door, or we'll get up in the morning and find our color TV set gone."

Being subjected to such racist conduct and beliefs at an impressionable age engendered in me hateful attitudes and thoughts about black people. My father was my first role model, and his example gave birth and contributed to my bias toward blacks.

One day my sister was walking down the street with two girls from the neighborhood. One was a black girl who lived a couple of blocks away on Del Rancho.

My father, who was out working in the garage, saw the girls. He stopped what he was doing and hollered at my sister, "You get over here right now!" When she did, my daddy began to scold her, screaming and yelling. "Don't you ever let me catch you walking around with them niggers." My father was furious at her.

I nodded in agreement, even though I didn't really know why. I just wanted to be like my dad. My rationalization was if daddy couldn't stand blacks then, by gosh, I wasn't going to like them either.

# Chapter Four

# A Seed of a Different Kind

After my father no longer let us ride the Sunday school bus, I began to attend church and Sunday school at Carter Park Baptist Church, which was across the street from my house. There I met the Sunday school teacher who would eventually have a great influence on my life.

Dave Edmondson planted in me the first real seed of truth concerning authentic Christianity and made the first major spiritual impact on my life. After I began attending Sunday school at Carter Park, Dave would come over, pick me up, and take me to church picnics. On these occasions he began to acquaint me with Jesus Christ, and I began to look up to him.

Dave showed me a different kind of love and attention than what I was accustomed to receiving.

At nine years old, I went forward in church for the first time, knelt at the altar, and asked Jesus into my heart. I came home, full of excitement, and told Daddy. His reaction was somewhat weird, if not mocking.

"Did you see the light?" he asked.

"What do you mean, see the light?"

"Well, when you ask Jesus into your heart, you are supposed to see a light coming toward you. You are supposed to see the light!"

He kept saying that again and again.

I thought he meant a real light actually coming down out of heaven. Although I didn't understand, I eventually convinced myself that I had seen this light in my mind.

I continued to tell Daddy about Sunday school, the activities we participated in, and how much I enjoyed it.

One day the preacher, the Reverend Bellomy, asked to come to our house for a visit. When Rev. Bellomy came over or when my Sunday school teacher Dave Edmondson stopped, Daddy would go out to the garage and start to work. He shut the garage door, indicating none too subtly that he did not want to be bothered. My mother explained to the pastor that my father was busy in the garage.

Daddy didn't want to talk to preachers — or Sunday school teachers.

Dave continued to spend a lot of time with me in those days, educating me in the stories of the Bible. Then one day I learned Dave had been in a motorcycle accident. As a result of the injuries, Dave died. My world, as I had known it, came crashing down. I was devastated.

After Dave's death, I did not care about going to church anymore because he was not there. I wondered why he had to die. I was confused, angry, and hurt. I could not bring myself to attend church anymore.

# Chapter Five

# A House Divided

After Dave Edmonson's death, it seemed my parents' fights grew worse. The drinking and the violence escalated. Sometimes they took their arguments outside.

The neighbor's children always were saying, "We saw your mom and dad outside in the yard fighting again."

Our tumultuous home life began to take its toll. My brother Larry left home at age 17 to join the army and was immediately assigned to Vietnam.

At age 16, my sister married a man named Bud Riley, a guitar player. I believe her main reason (at the time) for marrying him was to get out of the house and away from our parents. That left me and my little brother to contend with Dad and Mom.

One day my mother ran off with another man, claiming she was not coming back. She always came back, though. Why, I don't know.

"Why don't you just divorce Mom?" I used to ask Dad.

"I lost four sons in my first marriage because of divorce. I don't want to lose any more kids," he replied.

My father's first wife, Peggy, was from California. They had four boys, Bill, Bobby, Eddie, and Jerry, during their marriage. When Peggy and Dad divorced, she was given custody of the children. My father deeply regretted his failure to raise those boys and spend time with them. I guess that's why he was so determined to make his marriage to my mother work regardless of the fact they just did not get along well together.

In September 1970, my mom convinced my dad that she really was going to divorce him. Not too many days later I heard my mother screaming and crying. She frantically called for me, so I ran into the kitchen. "Johnny Lee, get out there in the garage and stop your daddy, stop your daddy!" I was stunned. What was I going to stop my daddy from doing?

I understood the urgency in my mother's voice so I hurried out to the garage through the kitchen door. It took my eyes a few moments to adjust to the dark garage. Finally, I distinguished my father's figure in the darkness as he leaned against the work table. I noticed something in his hand that he held to his head. As I drew closer I realized it was a gun.

My dad pointed the gun to his head and talked to himself. He was trying to convince himself that ending his life was the right thing to do.

I began to scream and cry out, "Daddy, don't do it! Daddy, don't kill yourself! I love you! I need you, Daddy. What would I do without you, Daddy? Please don't do this to yourself! Me and Terry Don need you. We don't want to grow up without a daddy. Daddy, please don't kill yourself!"

Daddy lowered the gun, grabbed me, and hugged me. He held me close for the longest time, tears rolling down his face. I did not think that he would ever do this again. I felt that he loved me too much. But my dad was under too much pressure, the kind of stress that I could never understand as a child. My father tried to conceal what he was going through, but I knew something was wrong.

We lived in a decent neighborhood, and we had a nice house. It was a brown ranch-style dwelling with three bedrooms. Daddy kept our home painted and clean. Both Mom and Dad loved flowers, so we always had a colorful array of them in the yard.

In the backyard Daddy also had a big garden with corn, watermelons, raspberries, and okra. My father loved working in the yard and took great pride in his garden. He was a hard worker who spent most of his life trying to achieve a measure of comfort.

Dad really tried to please my mother by providing all of her needs, but she took advantage of his kindness. Mother used, or rather abused, Daddy's credit cards to the point where she destroyed his credit. He eventually had to claim bankruptcy. Had I known all the pressures that my dad was under, I might have tried to be less of a trouble maker.

I was always in trouble in my neighborhood because I knew I could get away with it. I taught several neighborhood children how to curse. I stole my mother's cigarettes and smoked them. There I was, 11 years old, riding up and down the street on my bicycle smoking cigarettes. I didn't inhale. I was just blowing smoke, figuratively as well as literally. I thought I was something.

I often started fights with the neighborhood youngsters and wrote cuss words on the neighbors' cars. The neighbors sighed, "Here comes that little Johnny Lee again from down the street. He is always causing problems. We don't want him around our kids." I was very mean.

My role models were my parents — and they were always fighting — so what could anyone expect from me?

# Chapter Six

## Fallen Hero

On December 1, 1970, it all came to a head. I was 11 at the time, and Terry Don was seven. Early that night my dad called me into the bathroom while he was getting ready to go out.

"Son, there is something I have to tell you," he began. "I'm not going to be able to afford to give you and Terry Don a great big Christmas this year. I know you guys have been used to getting all kinds of presents. I wanted to see if it would be all right if I gave you my .410 shotgun and bought you a suit."

Looking at my daddy, my eyes began to brim with tears. "Daddy, I don't care about toys and stuff. I just want you. I love you, Daddy."

"Well, I love you too, son," he said. "Now, you watch your little brother. I'm going to go to the club." He left my brother and me there alone.

When my father came back from the nightclub he was visibly angry. He came to my door and asked, "Where is your mother? Have you seen her?"

"No, Daddy. I haven't seen her," I replied.

About that time my mother's friends, June and Jack, came into the house. I remember yelling at June and saying, "You leave my father alone! Haven't you caused enough problems around here already?"

She began to spew some very filthy words at me, words that are not even worth repeating. I stood my ground and began to yell back at her. I told June I didn't like her and to get out of our house. My father, who had been in the garage, heard the yelling and came in.

I was standing there arguing with June when my father ordered me into my bedroom. I went out of sight, but I didn't go to bed. I noticed that he had his pistol with him, his .45 automatic. I thought, Oh, he is going to get her. They started screaming at each other. During the altercation her husband Jack just sat there, saying, "Now why don't everybody just calm down?"

"You just shut your mouth if you know what's good for you," Daddy scowled at him.

Jack didn't say another word.

His wife June just kept yelling at my dad. She said my mother was leaving my father because he wasn't man enough to satisfy her. My dad said, "Well, I'm just going to kill myself." Some friends of the family, we called them Uncle Dale and Aunt Velma Davis, heard all the commotion and came across the street to try to calm everyone down.

My Uncle Dale talked soothingly to my father. "Look, Bill, you've been drinking. Let's put on a pot of coffee and we'll talk about it."

"Okay. I'll be over in a minute," Dad told Uncle Dale.

Uncle Dale and Aunt Velma left thinking that everything had calmed down. This would later prove to be far from the truth. I could tell that my daddy was getting more agitated.

Daddy told Jack, "You take your wife and you get out of here." But June kept saying that she wanted to take more of my mom's clothes. My dad was screaming at her, telling her to get out of his house.

Finally Dad announced: "I'm going to kill myself. I've had it."

"You don't have the guts to kill yourself," June countered. "You're gutless. You're not a man. You'll never amount to anything."

My dad turned around and he looked at her. He had this odd look in his eyes, a look I had never seen before. "Now, you don't think I'll do it." He put the gun to his head.

June was standing with the screen door open, and by this time I was standing right behind my father. Dad put the gun to his head and pulled the trigger. The whole top of his head came off. Blood splattered everywhere, including on me. He fell to the ground at my feet.

I began to scream and cry. I wanted to run but there was no place to go, so I stumbled against the wall. My little brother, who had been asleep in his bedroom, came out crying. I grabbed Terry Don by the hand, and we ran outside in the yard. The neighbors had heard the shot and run over. One of the neighbors took my brother and me into their house. We stayed there until the police came.

My mother had to be found. The sheriff eventually located her in a motel. He told her that Daddy was dying and she had to go with him to St. Anthony's Hospital in Oklahoma City. My father miraculously had lived through the night.

I walked into the intensive care unit and saw all those bandages and tubes all over my father's head as he lay there. I could not stand to look at him that way so I walked outside.

"Get this kid off the floor," one of the nurses said. "We can't have children up here."

"My father is in there, and I'm going to stay with him," I told her with determination.

Realizing that I was not going to leave, she went about her duties.

My mother finally showed up with the sheriff. I watched them as they came down the hall. She wouldn't even look at me. She asked a nurse, "Where is my husband?" They directed her to his room.

She walked through the door and went over to the side of the bed. As soon as she said, "Bill, it's me," lights on the machines began blinking frantically. Nurses and doctors came from all directions. They tried to revive him, but he was gone.

When Daddy died, I fell to the hospital floor, grabbed my stomach, and began to scream and cry. I knew that I wouldn't have anybody who loved me as much as my daddy. My idol had fallen. My hero had died.

My mother was so cold-hearted, she immediately wiped the tears from her eyes, fixed her clothes, and then demanded his car keys, his wallet, and his money. Then without saying a single word to me or anyone else, she left and rejoined her boyfriend.

Understandably, I had a lot of animosity toward my mother.

# Chapter Seven

# Like Father, Like Son

Not many days later, we had Daddy's funeral. My half-brothers came from California. I hadn't seen them for years. When the family returned from the funeral, there was nothing but arguing, fussing, and fighting.

Mom showed up at the funeral home with her boyfriend the day before the funeral. My half-brothers went after him, beat him up, and then chased him to the car and beat him some more. Mom screamed at them to stop. Someone had called the police. They arrived and broke up the fight. My mother's boyfriend jumped in his car and sped away.

About two or three days after the funeral, my mother moved her boyfriend into my father's house. My grandmother was going to live there with my mom to take care of us, but after a few days my mother got mad and threw her out.

After my grandmother moved out, all sorts of people started coming to the house to buy drugs. What troubled me the most, however, was that black people were coming too. My father would have never allowed this to happen. Back in 1970, integration hadn't taken place to the extent where blacks and whites were going in and out of each others' homes. We were in an all-white neighborhood filled with bigotry, prejudice, and racism.

All that I could think of at that point in my life was what Daddy had taught me. Even at my young age the seeds of racism had been deeply planted in me.

When black people came into the house to buy drugs from my mother, I stood up to them. I shouted at them and called them niggers, spades, spooks, jungle bunnies, or whatever derogatory name came to mind. And I told them to get out of my house.

They laughed at me and said, "You're just a little bigot."

One night when some blacks came to buy some drugs from my mother, I picked up the phone and called an uncle in Macon, Georgia. My uncle was a Ku Klux Klan member. It wasn't a secret; the whole family knew about it and was kind of proud of it.

I first heard the word Ku Klux Klan when he came to visit my father. I didn't know what the Ku Klux Klan was at that time, so I didn't really think anything of it. Later, it was explained to me that the KKK was an organization that kept the Negroes in their place. I thought it must be kind of like the Mafia, and you didn't mess with it. If you needed help, they would be there. Maybe one day I'll join, I thought.

"Can I come live with you?" I asked my uncle during one phone conversation.

"I'm sorry, Johnny Lee. I checked into bringing you and Terry Don to Georgia, but the judge said there was no way I could ever get custody of you."

"Mom has moved her boyfriend into the house, and blacks are coming here to buy drugs," I informed my uncle.

"Call your mother to the phone," he said tersely.

They got into a big shouting match while I listened on the other extension.

"If I come up there and find another man in my brother's house, they are going to have to carry him out feet first," he threatened.

My mother began to scream and call him all kinds of obscene names.

Needless to say, I received a terrible beating that night. Mother didn't beat me, but she allowed her friends to beat me. They hit me with shoes and everything else that they could get their hands on.

I went to school the next day but when classes ended, I rode the city bus to the nearest police station. I got off the bus and went in and told the police what had happened.

The police took me home so that they could talk to my mother. When we got to the house, my mother and her boyfriend were there. The policeman informed them that if he heard that someone had even touched me, he was going to put them both in jail.

When the police left, I was feeling kind of cocky. With a big smirk on my face I said, "You can't ever touch me again. If you do, I'll call the police on you."

My mother jumped up and said, "I don't care where you go or what you do, but you have got to get out of my life. I want you out of this house."

"Where will I go?" I asked.

"I don't know. That's up to you. Son or no son, you have to get out of here."

My mother gave me some money just to get rid of me, and I grabbed a suitcase and packed a couple pairs of pants and a shirt or two. I called all my relatives to see if I could stay with one of them, but none would take me. My mother would not let me stay with my grandmother for some reason. She just said, "You are not going to go stay with my mother either." I guess she just wanted me completely away from Oklahoma City.

As a last resort I called my sister in California and asked if I could come and stay with her. She said, "Okay."

At age 11, more alone than ever, I boarded a Greyhound bus and took an uncertain ride from Oklahoma to Long Beach, California.

# Chapter Eight

## In My Sister's House

Sandy and her husband Bud were living with Peggy, my father's ex-wife, when I arrived in California. That did not last long. At age 18, Sandy was in the midst of an affair with a man 20 years her senior. Not much time passed before Sandy left her husband for Richard Meye. This was like deja vu — my sister had begun to behave just like my mother.

Soon after moving to the West Coast, I began living with Sandy and Richard, and my life spun progressively more out of control. It often seemed that I was the only one looking out for me.

The one pleasure I looked forward to was my yearly, month-long visits with my grandparents and my little brother. Since my father had died my grandparents were the only people who made me feel loved and wanted. I always relished staying with them, but that month was just too short. I often wished that I could live with them all the time, but my sister would not hear of it.

My grandmother had a way of making me feel very special. She knew what I was going through, living with my sister, and she said, "Johnny Lee, we want you to come stay with us. We want to raise you."

My grandmother asked my sister for custody of me, but she refused. On one of my visits to northern California, she got on the phone with Sandy and tried again. "We'll file the necessary papers and do whatever it takes," she told Sandy. "All we want is for Johnny Lee to stay with us."

"No, I want him back here," Sandy insisted. "I have legal custody of him." The only reason she wanted me back was for the check that she received on my behalf each month. My grandmother could not afford to fight my sister in court, so I was sent back to Los Angeles.

When I got back, my sister had moved Richard into our apartment. Sandy told me to do whatever Richard said. Not bothering to even call me by my name, Richard referred to me as "punk." Sometimes he came in and said, "Hey, punk, did you take out that trash today?" If the trash had not been taken out, he would hit me in the mouth and pull my hair. Richard constantly told me that I was worthless and that I would never amount to anything.

One day he barked, "Hey punk, get downstairs and wash my car. Take these keys and back that car out — and you'd better wash and clean it right!" Being only 13 years old, I didn't know how to drive. When I backed that car out to wash it, I ran into a pole.

Richard ran down to the street, grabbed me by the hair, and pulled me out of the car. Then he started beating me. Kicking me in the mouth, he sent blood everywhere.

My sister came down to see what was happening. At first she protested, but she was also afraid of Richard so she could not stop it.

Sandy told me later to stay out of Richard's way. I gathered from this conversation that she backed him up.

"Why do you let him beat me like that?" I asked my sister.

"Because no one can control you but Richard. He will straighten you out and make a man out of you."

"I'm not putting up with this. I hate you guys!" I yelled.

Of course, she told Richard what I said and he gave me another beating. From then on I tried as much as I could to stay out of the house. The more I hung around there, the more I got beaten.

I missed my father. He never made me feel like I was irrelevant. He never beat me or called me names.

Remembering the good times I enjoyed with Daddy, I began to cry. I hurt because I wanted us to be like other families. I wanted to be like other kids who had parents who loved them and did not beat them. Watching children play little league baseball after school, I noticed their fathers cheering for them from the stands. I felt the sting of not having a father anymore.

# Chapter Nine

# Introduction to the Klan

I was at the point in my life where I really needed a father figure, and Richard was definitely not it. I felt the man hated my guts. I needed encouragement; I needed someone who was not going to beat me; I needed someone like my daddy. I concluded that the only people who loved and cared about me were my grandmother, grandfather, and my little brother. My own mother didn't care about me. I needed somebody to come into my life and to give me some sign of hope.

Reaching the ultimate low in my life, I felt completely alone. I really did not see any reason to live any more. I seriously contemplated killing myself. I needed someone to help me. Someone just to listen.

On this particular day in 1974, I had sunk to my lowest. Unable to deal with teachers or anyone else, I had stayed home from school.

While watching television, I heard David Duke talking about the Ku Klux Klan. He identified himself as the grand wizard of the Klan. He was only about 21 years old at the time, a very young guy. He was saying some of the same things that my father had said. That aroused my curiosity. I wrote down the address so that I could send for more information about the organization.

Hearing the phase "Ku Klux Klan" reminded me of my uncle and my father using those words during family gatherings. I listened intently as he talked about how blacks were trying to take over and how whites and blacks need to be separate. He sounded so much like my father that I felt this was someone with whom I needed to get acquainted.

I received some Klan literature in the mail shortly after seeing David Duke on television. The more I studied it, the greater my curiosity was aroused. I wanted to know as much as I could, but my zeal for knowledge had a horrible side effect. After reading this propaganda, I started having nightmares about blacks killing whites.

Not long after the information arrived in the mail, a man who looked to be my father's age came to our house. He asked for Johnny Lee Clary, which surprised me. No one ever came looking for me unless I was in trouble. Luckily, Sandy and Richard weren't at home. I opened the door to let this gentleman in the house, and he came in and shook my hand. Then he said, "I'm a friend of David Duke."

The man from the KKK gave me more brochures and papers about the Klan organization. He patted me on the back encouragingly and said, "You're a fine young man. You're going to go places in life, son. We were so proud that a young man like you would taken such an interest in God and His race and His nation. We are the true Christians, son. We're ordained by God to defend the white race. If you stay with us, you'll be a future leader of tomorrow. We're looking for young men like you who are willing to take up the torch and lead us into tomorrow for the future of this Aryan race."

I thought to myself, *Is this man for real?* Since my father's death no one had taken any interest in me. I was so vulnerable. *Finally*, I thought, *someone had seen that I was worth something.*

I was excited that this man wanted me to join the Klan youth core, and I eventually did. This happened the year I started high school at Bell Gardens High. One day at school, I shared with my class a newspaper article I had read about David Duke and the Ku Klux Klan coming through Los Angeles.

Then I told the class, "It's important for all the white Christians and all the white people to stand up and join us." I added the comment that "the only good nigger was a dead nigger."

The teacher stood up and countered what I had said.

"I don't feel like Mr. Clary does. We have to understand that there are a lot of rednecks in today's society, and it seems that we have one here."

He promptly sent me to the principal's office. The principal admonished me not to speak my views in class, but I was determined to recruit for the Klan. After this incident I became very unpopular at school. Everywhere I went students chided me, saying, "There goes the bigot." That didn't matter, however. I began to recruit with a vengeance throughout my entire time at this school.

The Klan meetings that I went to as a youth consisted of a bunch of good old boys sitting around hollering about black people until the wee hours of the night. Even though I never attended any mass Klan rallies as a youth, I was being groomed for future work in the Klan. I studied the books and read all the information and newspaper articles I could get my hands on. I went to meetings just to hear these older men talk about the glory days of the Klan. I began to attend mass meetings when I was 19.

While she was snooping around my room, Sandy found a stash of Klan literature. When I got home she confronted me.

"Johnny Lee, are you a member of the Klan?"

"I sure am. I joined it."

Sandy told her boyfriend Richard when he came home, and he blew his top. Of course, he beat me.

"I'll teach you to join the Ku Klux Klan!" Richard threatened. "You're just a little bigot, and I won't have any bigots living here."

Richard must have thought he could beat the desire for the Klan out of me. But as I lay on the floor with blood coming out of my mouth and nose, it didn't matter. I was more determined than ever to stay a part of the Klan. I didn't care; I hated Richard and I hated my sister for allowing him to beat me.

The Klan was my family now, and nothing would ever change that. My sister's protests and Richard's abuse couldn't dissuade me. Convinced that I was doing the right thing, I pursued my interest with even more vigor. In order to maintain the peace at home, however, I had to keep my involvement a secret.

# Chapter Ten

# Junior Recruiter

My junior year in high school marked a point in my life when things began to change drastically. My association with the Klan had made me a very unpopular kid on the campus. I wore a rebel flag and white power patches sewn to my jacket. Around the house I folded my jacket and carried it in such a way that Sandy and Richard wouldn't see the emblems. After leaving the house and disappearing from sight, I slipped into my jacket and headed to school.

As I began to make friends, things began to change a little. The racial mix at our school had changed a lot. More Mexicans lived in the city now, and some attended our school. I always had fights with them.

One particular fight in my sophomore year started while we were playing football in physical education class. A Mexican guy named Danny hit me in the mouth with a rock, knocking out several of my teeth. As I stood there with a mouth full of blood and teeth, he just laughed about it.

I swore I would get even with him. Several times I parked at the grocery store where he worked. One day I staked him out, getting ready to shoot him but people were around. I had the opportunity to get him later but decided against it.

I was constantly in fights because of my mouth, and my teeth usually paid the price. After getting hassled because I was often toothless, I eventually had my teeth redone. Not long after the dentist had completed his work, a street gang jumped me, pounded my head against the concrete, and messed up my mouth again. Since I could not afford to get them fixed again, I had to go around with messed up teeth while everybody made fun of the way I looked.

Nevertheless, I began to organize white students in my high school. "Do you see what's happening?" I asked them. "I've been telling you guys that they're taking over, but you haven't been listening to me. We've got to band together." Some of the white students began to listen to me. I continued, "This is why we have to have our own organization. We've got to stand up and show these Mexicans that they're not going to take over our schools."

Word got back to the Mexicans that we were attempting to expel their influence from our school. Since I led the organization, they went after me. One day a couple of Mexicans caught me alone and jumped me. I valiantly tried to defend myself. Suddenly, I glanced up and saw Mexicans flying all over the place. A big white guy was pulling the Mexicans off me. "You guys want a piece of me?" he bellowed. They apparently did not because they just took off running.

The guy who came to my rescue was named Leonard Kimble. We became best friends throughout high school. With all the hell I was experiencing at home, he was a welcome change for me. Leonard managed to keep me out of trouble most of the time. I liked having him around because he fought most of my battles. A wild kind of guy, Leonard was fun to be with, and we enjoyed each other's company.

He introduced me to pot and even made it seem like it was okay. He also introduced me to my first girlfriend. My junior year and that following summer were the best that I had since my father died. Unfortunately, Leonard graduated that next year, and I saw him only a few times after that.

As a Klan organizer, I was in charge of recruiting at high schools. Most of my rallies were in my own school. I was a constant trouble maker, always in the principal's office with several of my friends. School officials called Sandy a great deal, and I guess she grew weary of coming down to the school. They asked her for a solution to my problems. She suggested I join the army. Of course, I said no.

"You can go there or to juvenile hall," she said.

My hatred for my sister and her boyfriend grew with each passing day. I could not believe she was forcing me to choose between the army and juvenile hall. I wanted to stay home. Even though it was not the happiest place, it was home. Figuring I could handle it, I chose the army.

Taking the induction test at the army recruiter's office, I joined the army that same day. They sent me to Fort Knox, Kentucky in the fall of 1976. When I arrived, I had the shock of my life. I had never seen so many black people.

None of the films they had shown me at the recruiting station had any blacks in them. Those films depicted nothing but white officers and a white drill sergeant. I pictured the army as being all white. I didn't realize I would have to share my living quarters with black people. I couldn't believe it.

To my surprise and discomfort, black drill sergeants were everywhere. They would get in my face, yell at me, and call me names. *This is crazy,* I thought to myself, *I'm not going to allow this.* I began to rebel. One of the black drill sergeants quickly sensed my defiance.

"All right, Clary. Drop and give me 20 pushups."

"You drop and give me 20," I replied. "I'm not doing anything you tell me to do. This is a white person you're talking to."

"What did you say to me?" he asked incredulously.

Of course, I repeated myself. So he sent me to see the Commanding Officer.

"Son, what is your problem?" asked the C.O.

"The problem's not with me; it's with those people," I replied.

"What do you mean, 'those people'?"

"The niggers," I said.

"The niggers?"

"Yeah, that's why us white guys gotta stick together. Listen, I don't know about you, but I belong to a group called the Ku Klux Klan back home. We don't allow some of the things you allow those niggers to get away with."

While I spoke he took his pencil and wrote bigot across my file in huge letters.

"Son, when you join the army you look to the man on your left and you look to the man on your right and if you see any color other than green, you are not fit for today's army. I'm gonna put your butt in jail."

"Jail! For what? What offense have I committed?"

"Becoming a bigot."

I was placed under guard because the Commanding Officer said some blacks wanted to kill me. Word traveled quickly that I was a racist Klan member who had told off the drill sergeant and called him a nigger. My very presence caused a lot of tension and chaos on the base.

Finally, I was brought before the C.O. again. I had heard the army was going to discharge me, and I figured that it would be dishonorable.

"Why is the army giving me a dishonorable discharge if I was just stating my beliefs?" I asked.

"We are going to give you an honorable discharge and put you out of the army," the C.O. replied. "Your papers will say that you were marginal and nonproductive. You will be ineligible to join any armed services for the next two years. You've gotta lot of growing up to do, kid."

The military kept me in protective custody for two weeks while they processed my paperwork, and then they escorted me off the base. They asked me where I wanted to go. I knew I couldn't go back to Bell Gardens or put up with Sandy and all those problems. I thought of my older brother Larry whom I hadn't seen in years. We had never been close when we were kids, but I decided to visit him.

Larry lived in Kansas at the time. We started fighting our first evening together. We argued about everything, but mostly we clashed about our different views on the military. For seven years Larry had made a career out of the army, attaining the rank of sergeant. He could not understand why I had left the service.

Johnny Lee Clary (1 year old) with
his father in Del City, OK. May 1960.

My grandmother, Mrs. Mamie "Nan-Nan" Carter.

Johnny Lee Clary as leader of the Oklahoma State KKK. 1980.

Johnny Lee Clary with former Imperial Wizard, Bill Wilkinson, re-cruiting high school students for the KKK in front of Moore High School in Moore Oklahoma. January 1980.

Johnny Lee Clary speaking at a KKK rally.  September 1988.

Another night out with the boys in the hoods.

Rev. Wade Watts, Clary's old rival, is now one of his best friends. Wade Watts is the uncle of U.S. Congressman J.C. Watts of Oklahoma. 1992.

Tia Watts as a child.

Tia Watts graduated from high school as class valedictorian in June of 1994.

Johnny Lee Clary with former N.W.A. World Wrestling Champion, Nature Boy Buddy Landell. June 1994.
(Johnny, a former professional wrestler, held the Arkansas Heavy Weight Championship title three times, before retiring from wrestling in 1988)

Johnny Lee Clary as "Johnny Angel," Arkansas Heavy Weight Champion with his ring valet Miss Becky Starr. May 1987.

Johnny Lee Clary with Juan Juarez, pastor of Valley
Faith Fellowship in Delano CA, and Geraldo Rivera
in New York City. January 1995.

Johnny Lee Clary with Roy Ennis, president of CORE (Congress of Racial Equality), who was involved in the famous brawl with Skin-Heads on The Geraldo Show in October 1988. This photo was taken in January 1995 when Johnny and Roy teamed up to face Tom and John Metzger on The Geraldo Show.

Johnny Lee Clary with Phil Donahue and Rev. Wade Watts in New York. Johnny and Rev. Watts took on the KKK on Donahue's show and "steam rolled" them, making the Klan members look like fools. April 1995.

Johnny Lee Clary with movie star and comedian, Jackie Mason, in New York City. Jackie, who is Jewish, befriended Johnny since they both share an interest in overcoming racism.  April 1994.

Johnny Lee Clary with his high school best friend, Leonard Kimble, in Azusa, CA. This photo captures the first time Johnny had seen Leonard in 17 years.

Johnny Lee Clary with Carlton Pearson, a well-known TV Evangelist, who helped Johnny get started in the ministry and remains close friends with him to this day.

Johnny Lee Clary with Ben Kinchlow, co-host of The 700 Club. 1994.

Johnny Lee Clary with Pat Robertson on The 700 Club. 1994.

Johnny Lee Clary with former Charles Manson Family member, Susan Atkins, author of "Child of Satan - Child of God." Susan is also a former white supremacist who is now a born again Christian. Today Johnny and Susan are close friends.

Johnny Lee Clary with Dr. Jerry Saville.  August 1994.

Johnny Lee Clary with Dr. Phillip Goudoux, former Minister of Defence of The Black Panther Party who is now a born again Christian. He pastors Calvary Christian Center in Sacramento, CA. August 1994.

Johnny Lee Clary with close friends Jeff and Reeni Fenholt on TBN's "Praise the Lord" program. Jeff Fenholt is a former member of the rock group "Black Sabbath." He had the starring role in the hit Broadway musical, "Jesus Christ Superstar."

Larry accused me of being no better than a draft dodger. He told me that he had plenty of black friends while he was in the army. He could not and would not understand my racism. Feeling unwelcome in his home, I left after a month.

I returned to Bell Gardens, California and got an apartment there. I began to run around with my buddy Leonard. We were partying, smoking pot, and chasing girls.

Leonard's aunt and uncle were pastors of Bell Gardens Church of God. Leonard's parents served as deacons there. He went to church, but after the service we got together to party. I accompanied Leonard to church and even made some friends there.

Not really wanting to attend church, I did some pretty outrageous things. I ordered some T-shirts that said "Secret Member of the KKK," which I wore to church. Sometimes I slipped Klan propaganda into the offering plate. Pastor Marvin Cain, Leonard's uncle, told me on more than one occasion that his patience was wearing thin with me. A few people at the church had labeled me a trouble maker, suggesting to the pastor that I be kicked out. Pastor Cain would not hear of it, but I know the thought must have crossed his mind.

One Sunday night I heard the assistant pastor, the Rev. Bill Means, preach a sermon called "A Heartbeat From Heaven." That sermon really got to me. I felt the urgency to change my way of living. I went to the altar, knelt down, and began to pray.

Pastor Cain, who was sitting in the front row, came and knelt beside me and began to pray. Pastor Means began to weep, as did almost the entire church. Many of them had prayed for me without ceasing. I got up from that altar feeling like a new person. I woke up the next morning thinking, *Wow! I'm really a Christian now!*

Unfortunately, my excitement wore off after a few weeks. Before that night I always dated "party girls" from the church who were not saved, and I soon grew tired of them. My eyes were on two girls at the church who were real Christians: Donna Gravett and Kim Smith. Every time I asked either of them out, they refused because I was not a Christian. Now I was excited about the possibility of a relationship with these girls.

After a few weeks, I asked Donna out and was turned down flat. I comforted myself by saying, "There's always Kim." Kim had dated Leonard for a while, but their relationship had ended. I decided to make my move on Kim, but she rejected me also.

A hell raiser and a party boy, my friend Billy always had the "bad girls" with him. He was mad at me for a few weeks after I got saved and started going to church. As soon as he found out that I had been rejected by both girls, however, he came around with some of his wild girlfriends and invited me to join them. I was feeling very low at the time. What the heck, I decided, I might as well have some fun. So I joined them.

A little while later on Halloween night, Billy and I were driving around town throwing eggs at people's houses and cars. I had been dared to egg Pastor Means' house, and after a couple of beers I decided to go for it. We circled his house twice, and each time we hit it with eggs. Pastor Means came out and chased us down the street.

Someone called the police, and they caught us later that night. The officers hauled us out of the car and made us break all our eggs. One of the policemen told us that if he heard of anything we had done, he would personally arrest us.

I got home that night in one piece, but I woke up the next morning with a major hangover. Beer cans were strewn all over the apartment. Someone was pounding on my front door with a vengeance. I gathered my wits and stumbled to answer the door.

There stood Pastor Means. Brushing past me without even a good morning, he said, "Johnny Lee, I urge you to repent and ask the Lord to forgive you. Why don't we pray right now?"

"No, I like to party," I replied. "Being a Christian is boring. I'm young and I have a lot of living to do."

He sat down and began to weep. Without another word, he stood to leave. He strode to the door, turned, and said, "I'll be praying for you." With that he left. After I shut the door behind him, I really felt bad.

A couple months later, I decided to return to Oklahoma. My grandparents and my brother Terry Don had already moved back to Oklahoma. They had been living in Martinez, California. I decided to follow them.

The Bell Gardens Church of God took up a collection and gave me about $100 for traveling money. Despite how I had treated them, they still cared about me. That was real love. Seventeen years passed before I would see any of them again.

# Chapter Eleven

## On My Own

I found my own place to live and got a job pumping gas at a service station. After work, it was party time. I would come home and sleep until late in the afternoon.

One day my grandfather picked me up from work because my car had broken down. As I climbed into the back seat, he said to my brother, "Let Johnny Lee be a lesson to you to stay in school. He dropped out and now he is rolling around in grease for $2.00 an hour. He will never amount to anything."

I felt sad and wondered why my grandfather disliked me so much. None of my older siblings had finished high school. I would have been just like them had it not been for my grandfather's comment. After I thought about it for a while, I decided I would show him. In the fall of 1978, I enrolled in Del City High School to finish my senior year.

Because I started recruiting other kids to join the Klan within a few weeks of my arrival, I soon found myself in the principal's office. When administrators received my school records from Bell Gardens, California, they learned I had caused a great deal of racial tension. School officials were not happy to have me around.

While in the principal's office I shared one of my many escapades. I had organized a race riot while attending high school in California. A white kid had been jumped and stabbed by a gang of Mexicans. I stirred up the white kids on campus to take revenge by having a rumble with the Mexicans.

About 200 white boys and girls followed me to the middle of campus to fight. At least 200 Mexicans stood ready. Just as we were about to begin this big fight, the police charged in and everybody ran away. I was later identified as the ring leader.

The principal at Del City High School informed me that he would not tolerate any of those antics at his school. Needless to say, a couple of weeks later I wore a KKK T-shirt to school and was promptly expelled. I was to be transferred to Midwest City High School, the rival school. I started partying and eventually dropped out for about three weeks. Mr. Vann, a teacher at Midwest City High School, encouraged me to return to school. Had it not been for his en-

couragement, I would not have gone back and graduated that year.

One winter night my friends and I were hanging
out in my apartment. We were bored and looking
for trouble. Someone found out that a group of Indians were having a party in the next apartment
complex.

"This is white power country!" one of the guys
boasted.

"What are we going to do about it?" I asked the
group. I really didn't want a whole lot of trouble; I
was only interested in partying. But I was good at
getting the guys hyped up.

Amid the bantering, two or three of the guys left
without my realizing it. Twenty minutes later, they
ran back to the apartment and banged on the door
for us to let them in.

"What happened?" I asked as they burst through
the door.

"We went to the apartment complex where the
Indians were and busted out the windows in their
cars," they gasped. They tried to get away without
being seen, but several Indians came after them with
baseball bats.

I looked out the window and saw at least 25 people
with bats. There were about 20 of us, mostly girls, in
the apartment. We decided to take them head on,
so we charged outside. The battle raged. People were
screaming, and fists and bats were flying. I was swing-

ing at every Indian I could see. Finally, we had the upper hand, and the Indians began to retreat.

One Indian man, however, remained cornered by a couple of the guys. He pulled a gun and started firing. I think he thought he hit me because I slipped on the ice and fell. He took off running. The police came and we all ran.

When I finally arrived back at my apartment, I discovered it almost totally destroyed. Needless to say, I had to move. I was really making a name for myself.

I found another apartment and began to concentrate on recruiting for the Klan. I realized I could not afford to get into too much trouble and be an effective KKK recruiter. As it turned out, I was a great recruiter for the Klan. I put ads in newspapers and set up phone hotlines.

A reporter from the Oklahoma newspaper called and asked why I was using the newspaper to propagate hate. Then the reporter asked me questions about myself. The next day's front page headline read, "Klan Recruiter Launches Citywide Drive." The article mentioned that I would be recruiting at the high schools, as well as enlisting adults.

I started getting all kinds of calls from people honestly interested in the Klan. As a result of the response from the telephone hotline and the newspaper article, I launched a massive recruiting mission. I went to candidates' homes, to restaurants, everywhere possible to meet conscripts.

Pretty soon the media started following my every move. Reporters showed up at high schools where I was recruiting and at Klan youth rallies. I could always count on the media to be there.

Once I went to Mid West City High school and took several young recruits with me. I called the media myself this time because I wanted them there. Armed with lots of Klan information to distribute, I wanted to make the most of this event.

The media showed up in full force — and so did the police. The officers harassed me and the rest of the group. They really did not have anything for which to arrest me, but they gave me a ticket for a noisy muffler on my car. They told us to leave or they would try to find something to run us in for.

Needless to say, we left without conducting the rally, yet we still succeeded in recruiting several youth. Later we went to my little brother's school to recruit. This time the media came uninvited. My little brother was having a ball; he enjoyed the attention that he received.

Unfortunately, my grandfather saw the Klan rally on the news that night. Terry Don had a cigar in his mouth, talking about the Klan and how he welcomed them to his school. He was 16 years old at the time and still living with my grandparents. My grandfather exploded. He threatened to whip my brother and take his car away from him. Terry Don didn't have much to do with the Klan after that incident.

# Chapter Twelve

## Bill and Me

I decided to move to the Oklahoma City area and recruit for Bill Wilkinson and his Klan. I was no longer with David Duke because our views about the Klan conflicted. Duke, who long held ambitions to run for president, seemed more interested in politicking and women. He preached a message of nonviolence, proclaiming that the Klan could take control of the country by the ballot box.

While working as Duke's bodyguard one day, I got into a fight with Duke in a restaurant about my calling a group of black people niggers. It seemed to me that no one would join the Klan and associate it with nonviolence.

One night in early 1979, I received an unexpected call from Bill Wilkinson's people. They told me that Bill Wilkinson, the imperial wizard for the United States, was interested in talking to me. The news surprised me and also made me somewhat anxious.

The next night I reached Bill Wilkinson and announced who I was.

He said, "I've been getting calls from several reporters talking about you and all the recruiting that you've been doing for me. I just wanted to talk to you myself. It sounds like you've started a good thing here in our area. I want to come up there for a visit. You can pick me up at the airport." He told me he would come from Louisiana and help get things organized.

Bill's planned visit filled me with excitement. I called everybody and told them he was coming to town. Just before he arrived, a race riot broke out between blacks and whites in Idabell, Oklahoma. A white security guard shot a black youth who supposedly was trying to steal something from a car outside a bar.

The town was going up in flames. Whites were shooting blacks, and blacks were shooting whites. The media got wind of Bill's arrival, and they came out in force to meet him at the airport. When I got to the airport, people were everywhere.

When Bill stepped off the plane, I was the first person to meet him. After our brief introduction, he instructed me to flank him on his right side. Then he directed me to a wall to have an impromptu press conference.

"Mr. Wilkinson, do you plan to visit the riot area?" a reporter asked.

"Yes, we will!" he replied.

I stood there dumbfounded. I had no intentions of going down to Idabell, Oklahoma, where they were rioting.

We had a meeting that night, and he laid out his plan of action and his itinerary. At this meeting he named me state kleagle, which means state organizer or public relations man. Bill Wilkinson informed me that I was too young, at age 19, to be leading adults. His comment offended me. I felt that I was capable to run the Klan, but I didn't want to push the issue.

Some of the adults in the Klan certainly did have a problem, in more ways than one. One night outside Idabell, in a park known as Talamena Drive, some klansmen got drunk and decided to throw watermelons at black people. After donning their sheets, a bunch of them climbed into the back of a pickup truck. Packed with klansmen, the pickup drove down the main drag in Idabell, where the blacks hung out. The klansmen started hurling watermelons at the black people, while playing "Dixie" on the P.A. system.

After an hour of watermelon throwing, the boys decided that this was too much fun to stop. They wanted to do it again. I told everyone that the worst thing we could do was return to the scene of the crime. Of course they didn't listen.

They drove back into town with "Dixie" blasting over the P.A. system. They had their watermelons ready, but this time the black people were waiting for them. They came out throwing rocks, tomatoes, eggs, and anything else they could get their hands on!

When someone hurled a rock into the windshield, the klansman who was driving lost control and nearly overturned the truck. One klansman fell off the back of the truck. He got up and started running down the street. Having packed his shotgun with rock salt, a black man shot him in the butt.

We slowed down just long enough to pick him up, and then we sped off into the night. The klansman with the rock salt in his behind knew he could not go to the hospital because the sheriff was looking for us. So he had to let his wife pick the salt out of his butt.

Not long after that, we went down to Idabell, Oklahoma. It was horrible. Fires had gutted homes and businesses everywhere. It looked like a war zone. The devastation shocked me. Just being there made me very uncomfortable.

Wilkinson, in his three-piece suit and with a cigar shoved into his mouth, announced, "We have come here to put niggers in their place." The highway patrol escorted us in because threats had been made on Wilkinson's life, as well as my own. We ended up playing cat-and-mouse with the police all day. We had tried to have a meeting but could not because the police kept tailing us everywhere we went. Eventually, we left slightly disappointed.

Around this time I had met a young girl named Cindy who said she had seen my newspaper ads. She shared with me her commitment to the white race and how much she had always admired the KKK. By that comment I should have known that something was up.

Smitten by her good looks, I didn't use good judgment. I began to fall in love with her. Many of the Klan members didn't trust her and said that I shouldn't trust her either. But you know the old saying, "Love is blind." I was definitely blind. Later I discovered she was sent to infiltrate the Klan. She had orders to get as much information as possible about us.

My eyes were not opened until Cindy decided to go after a bigger fish. She dumped me and began having an affair with Bill Wilkinson. It did not seem to matter to either of them that Wilkinson was married and had children in Denham Springs, Louisiana. He had played right into her hands.

Until that point, I had viewed Bill Wilkinson as sort of a superman of the Klan. He was nothing like David Duke, who had taken the weaker stance. "We are nonviolent people," Duke said. On the other hand, Wilkinson boasted, "We are violent. If you attack us, we are going to attack back." I had often thought to myself, *If my dad were alive he would have liked Bill Wilkinson.* But now I saw a different side to my Klan leader. Wilkinson was a snake to me.

There was no way I could trust him anymore after what had happened, and I definitely could not trust Cindy. What kind of family man was he? How could he cheat on his wife — with my girlfriend? I thought we were friends.

Despite my anger over being betrayed, I didn't want to confront him because I had a good thing going. Now in charge of the Klan in my area, I didn't want to lose it all. Cindy was dangerous, and I was going to let him hang himself.

# Chapter Thirteen

# "Loving Thy Neighbor"

Not long after the situation with Bill and Cindy, I met a man who would impact my life greatly.

As I sat home one night, a former girlfriend called to inform me that a radio station was talking about me. I turned on the radio and found a live talk show being broadcast nationwide. Sure enough, the topic for the evening featured the Klan and me.

I called in to say a few words on behalf of the Klan. The station was surprised to hear from me, as I knew they would be. Listeners started calling in to talk to me. I talked for about 10 minutes to different people, answering many of their questions.

When the program ended, the host asked me if I would be a guest on his talk show the following Sunday night. I agreed, thinking this would be a prime opportunity to talk about the Klan. The entire two hours would be mine.

Thrilled at my good fortune, I called everyone I knew and told them I was going to be on the radio. A little while later, while driving around the city and listening to the radio, I heard a commercial that stunned me. The station announced a debate between Johnny Lee Clary, leader of the Ku Klux Klan, and the Rev. Wade Watts, head of the National Association for the Advancement of Colored People.

When I heard this, I almost wrecked my car. "I'm going to debate who? I never agreed to debate anyone!" Trying to find a pay phone, I drove like a mad man. "This has to be a mistake! Why would I want to debate a nigger?"

Finally finding a phone, I immediately called the radio station. I informed the person receiving the call that I never agreed to any debate. I was very angry, so angry that the person on the other end of the line could not get a word in. Finally, I calmed down long enough to listen to what was being said. After a lengthy discussion, I finally agreed to do the debate.

I had never had a face-to-face debate with a black man. I had always had it out with them at some time or another, but this would be different.

The day finally arrived, and I was nervous about the confrontation. I sat in the studio in quiet anticipation. I expected Rev. Watts to show up wearing an African dashiki and sporting an Angela Davis-size Afro. I just knew he would flash his switchblade in one hand and in the other hold a boom box blaring music from Shaft.

I was not prepared for what I saw.

As I sat there waiting for the show to start, I glanced toward the door and in walked a well-dressed black man wearing a suit and tie and carrying a Bible. He approached me, extended his hand, and said, "Hello, Mr. Clary. My name is Reverend Wade Watts, and I just want to tell you that I love you and Jesus loves you."

I didn't know how to react. Even though Klan rules forbid shaking a black man's hand, I reached out and clasped his hand. Then I looked at my palm, still in shock that I actually shook hands with a black man.

"Don't worry; it won't rub off," Rev. Watts quipped.

*This man even has a sense of humor,* I said to myself. I couldn't understand why this man treated me so nicely. I really expected Rev. Watts to show animosity toward me.

I had accompanied Bill Wilkinson on a couple of programs where he had debated Senator E. Melvin Porter and a couple other black leaders in Oklahoma.

They all showed open enmity toward him, and that's what I expected from Rev. Watts. When he did not, I was caught off guard.

Rev. Watts explained when the NAACP was founded and its mission. Then the host turned the microphone to me, and I described the Klan. I outlined its aims, goals, and objectives.

"Why is there a need for the Klan in Oklahoma?" the host asked.

"Well, the white people want some relief. They are tired of the races mixing, and blacks and whites intermarrying," I replied, trying unsuccessfully to insult Rev. Watts.

"Why do you feel that way?" the host prompted me.

"Blacks and whites should not intermarry because blacks aren't good enough to marry whites. There is an obvious difference between the races. I think the Bible speaks against racial intermarriage," I added for the Reverend's benefit.

"What scriptures support your assertion?" Rev. Watts quickly asked.

"I don't know where it is in the Bible," I began. "I didn't bring a Bible with me."

"You're welcome to use mine."

"Thank you, Rev. Watts, but I don't know exactly where it is. But somewhere in the Bible isn't there a verse that says, 'What fellowship hath light with darkness?'"

He looked at me like I was nuts.

"You have totally misquoted the Bible," he said, pointing me to Numbers 12. "Have you ever heard of Moses?"

"Yes, I have heard of Moses."

"What color would you say an Ethiopian woman was?"

"Black."

"Moses married an Ethiopian woman in Numbers 12, and his sister Miriam spoke out against it. This angered God so much that He smote her with leprosy. If God did that to Miriam, imagine what He's going to do to you!"

"Now wait a minute," I blurted. "I don't like that, Reverend Watts! It is just not right for blacks and whites to intermarry. You're all monkeys," I said, insinuating that he was not even human. "Your race hung out in trees, ate your brothers, and threw coconuts at each other."

Rev. Watts countered, "You know, John, cats will have kittens; chickens will have chicks; horses will have colts; but monkeys will have little monkeys and human beings will have babies. A human being cannot have a monkey, and a monkey cannot have a human being. I am a human being."

"We should go back to segregated schools. Negroes aren't as smart as white people," I asserted, wanting the Reverend to feel inferior.

"What do you base that upon?" he asked.

"William Shockley and Arthur Jensen, two Ivy League-educated professors, together developed an intelligence test on which the average black scored 15 percent lower than the average white. What do you have to say to that?" I challenged him.

"What color were the men who wrote the test?" he asked.

"What difference does that make?"

"It makes all the difference in the world," he replied. "I'll give you a test right now and, believe it or not, I could flunk you."

"You cannot flunk me because I am more intelligent than you."

He was equally as emphatic. I finally consented to taking his test.

"All right, prepare to answer. How long is the average roach? Do roaches walk or do they fly? How long does it take for a mess of chitlins to cook? How do you kill rats in the ghetto? Can you kill them with a Coca Cola? How do you pickle pigs' feet?"

"Now just hold on a minute," I said. "White folks ain't supposed to know the answers to questions like that. Those questions are for your people to know.

You can't ask a white person questions like that. What's the matter with you? You rigged that!"

He looked me squarely in the eyes and said, "Bingo, you've got it. Now what do you think of your Professor Jensen and your Professor Shockley?"

I didn't realize it at the time, but I had just been made a fool of over national radio. Trying to redeem myself, I quoted Thomas Jefferson. David Duke had printed literature that said Thomas Jefferson advocated keeping the races pure and promoted superiority of the white man.

"While Jefferson may have said those things, he did not practice them," Rev. Watts said. "Let me give you a quick history lesson, John. Thomas Jefferson and his black mistress, Sally Hemmings, produced quite a few children. So what do you mean by quoting Thomas Jefferson?"

Our dialogue couldn't be edited. I was looking more and more like an idiot on live, national radio. *This guy is something else,* I thought. I didn't realize he would be so intelligent. Not only was I losing the debate, I was losing badly.

As I was leaving the studio, Rev. Watts stood in the lobby with several people.

"Hold on, Mr. Clary, just a minute," he said. "I want to leave you with this thought. I want you to know no matter what you do to me, no matter what you say to me, you can't do enough to me to make me hate you. I'm going to keep praying for you."

Then he held up an 18-month old baby girl who was half white and half black.

"This is the very thing that you despise, and this is the very thing that you spoke out against. This is my adopted daughter. Her daddy was black; her mother was white. Neither one of the kids' families wanted her, so I adopted the baby. This is my baby!"

The Reverend continued, "I want you to look into these sweet, innocent eyes and tell me how you can hate this baby. She can't help it that she was born into the world like that, but she's beautiful, John. You tell me how you can hate her. This child couldn't do anything to harm you; she couldn't do anything to hurt you; she does not know hate."

When I looked at the baby, her eyes met mine. She stared at me as if to say, "Why hate me? What did I ever do to you?"

My heart began to ache, and I turned around.

"I can't talk to you anymore," I said as I stomped out of the studio.

The image of that baby stayed in my mind as the years passed. When I spoke against interracial marriage and talked about how evil it was for blacks and whites to intermarry, I relived the encounter with this little baby. I even dreamed about that baby on several occasions.

After the debate the Klan stepped up its attack on Rev. Watts by, among other things, harassing him and calling him names over the telephone. I was one of those who made threatening phone calls. Klansmen often marched in front of his house in the middle of the night wearing their sheets and hoods.

Rev. Watts called the sheriff to report the activity. Generally, though, the sheriff merely asked, "Well, are they doing anything to you? If not, they have just as much a right to walk the streets as you do." Rev. Watts had to call the highway patrol to escort his children to school because the sheriff would not do it.

The Klan also set fire to his church. Klansmen wanted to have a rally and burn a cross about a mile from his home, but Rev. Watts went to court and got an injunction against them. Instead of the cross burning that night, we set the Reverend's church on fire. The fire was extinguished before it completely destroyed the edifice.

Despite the hate and vandalism, whenever I called to harass him, he said, "I know who this is, and I'm still praying for you." This man had a way of unnerving me. The Klan was terrorizing his family and calling him every name in the book, but this man of God refused to hate and lower himself to the same level to which the klansmen and I had stooped.

During this time, Cindy was still trying to set me up. She also knew I suspected her real motives. Having collected enough evidence to convict her as an infiltrator, I called Klan court and a Klan tribunal on her. They voted to banish Cindy from the Klan and to harass her for the rest of her life. Cindy was served with banishment papers, which meant she was viewed as an outcast and enemy of the group.

She then called Bill Wilkinson, the imperial wizard, and told him what happened. Of course, Wilkinson called me and said I had rigged the court. There was no way he was going to have Cindy banished from the Klan. The incident generated more discord and increased the infighting. Soon the Klan factions were at war with one another.

# Chapter Fourteen

## Apostle of Hate

At this time I went to Southwest High School to recruit. Cindy discovered my plans and called the news media. When we arrived, a big anti-Klan rally was underway on the campus. A bunch of students jumped on my car and broke the windows. I knew better than to hit a kid with the cameras rolling, even though I wanted to. The rally made the Klan look really bad.

Cindy sent a friend of hers from the newspaper to interview me. I used part of the interview to denigrate Bill Wilkinson and bragged that Wilkinson could not stop me from recruiting high school students. Of course this got back to him.

Wilkinson called me and said, "Look, Clary, the organization has had it with you. You are no longer a Klan leader. The other leaders and I are going to bring you down. Cindy brought treason charges against you for speaking against the imperial wizard in the interview. A Klan court will be held on the matter."

I stood my ground against Wilkinson.

"You don't need to hold court. I'm resigning from your organization."

"You can't quit," he responded.

Not only did I leave, but I formed the independent Knights of the Ku Klux Klan and took many of Wilkinson's members with me.

I decided I needed the backing of a national organization and soon became aware of Tom Metzger, who had just won the democratic nomination for congressman in Orange County, California with 55,000 votes. His election in the summer of 1980 made national headlines. He seemed like the type of man we needed as our wizard, and someone from whom I could receive input and guidance. I enjoyed a large following in Oklahoma, but Tom Metzger was known nationally.

After some investigating I found out where Tom lived. When we met, I explained what I was doing in Oklahoma and what had happened with Wilkinson. Metzger knew what was going on because Wilkinson had come to California and tried to bust up his Klan and raid his membership.

Metzger was associated formally with David Duke but had grown disgusted with him. It seems Duke made light of an announcement by California klansmen that they were going to patrol the borders to keep illegal aliens from entering the United States. The patrol announcement made national headlines. Metzger brought Duke to California and had arranged for media to be there. They announced that they were bringing in the grand wizard himself, David Duke.

When Duke deplaned, however, he seemed more concerned with getting laid than with responding to the media attention. Instead of talking to the media about patrolling the border, Duke looked around, took off his sunglasses, and said, "Hey, Tom, where are all the women? Fix me up. I need a girl for the night." Tom exploded, and he ended his working relationship with David Duke.

Many of the members, national as well as local, greatly respected Tom and looked to him as their leader. After that incident, Tom reorganized the Knights of the Ku Klux Klan into the California Knights of the Ku Klux Klan. He declared his organization independent for the State of California, where he then proceeded to fight communist demonstrators and the International Committee against Racism.

Tom ridded his members of their sheets and hoods and replaced them with black helmets, black pants, and black shirts. He armed his members with shields and baseball bats and commanded them to take the battle to the streets. Whenever this new breed of klansmen conducted rallies or terrorized civil demonstrations, they jumped on the demonstrators, assaulting them verbally and physically. Tom was a very tough, cold-hearted person and fellow klansmen respected him for that.

I was looking for experienced guidance, and Metzger appeared to be the man who could give it to me. I had a lot of members throughout Oklahoma, and I was quickly becoming very powerful in the ranks of the KKK organization. My youth and inexperience at independent leadership also dictated that I needed the wisdom of the fathers of my faith — that faith being allegiance to the white race and the KKK movement and agenda. I knew only with that wisdom would I be able to rebuild the organization into one that was mighty in its strength, ability, and willingness to uphold what I thought then to be the exclusive superiority of the white race.

In July 1980, I met face-to-face with Metzger after locating his residence in Fallbrook, California. When I arrived at his house, his wife met me at the door and welcomed me. Tom came out, and I introduced myself and told him why I was there. We talked for a while and then he invited me to dinner.

We sat down at the table as his wife treated us to a southern pot roast meal. Once the food was served, Tom prayed over the dinner. That really impressed me at the time. I thought, *Wow! Metzger is a Christian!*

After dinner we continued to talk. I knew Metzger was a man who meant business. I told him what my intentions were and what I wanted with the Klan in Oklahoma. He responded that at this time we should keep our Klans independent of each other, because he had all he could handle with California and he was not prepared to branch out nationally. Then he gave me some advice.

"I suggest you get rid of those white sheets and organize your people. If you go out on the street demonstrating, wear street clothes so you can fight easily in the event that you are attacked. I'll help you all I can. If you need literature, if you need newspapers, I'll send you whatever I can. If you ever need advice, you know you can give me a call." This was the beginning of a long relationship.

When I arrived back in Oklahoma, I talked with Lou, the first police officer whom I had met in Oklahoma City (Some of my first recruits were police officers). I told him about my encounter with Metzger. Lou agreed that we should build an independent Klan. We began to have meetings, and I began to compile our own literature. I wrote Metzger to get other pamphlets and information.

During this time I found out that Cindy was blackmailing Bill Wilkinson. Many of his members were calling us, saying, "John, you were right. We shouldn't have stayed with Bill Wilkinson. Something's going on between Bill and Cindy. Bill has set Cindy up in an apartment. He pays her rent and gives her money."

Cindy caused problems between many of the klansmen. She was sleeping with several of them, and their wives were finding out. Now everyone was at each others' throats; all hell was breaking loose.

Cindy worked for the *Daily Oklahoman* newspaper. I always wondered if she was a reporter working undercover, but she always insisted that she worked in the classified ad section. One night a group of my Klan brothers and I talked about the things Cindy had done. "Someone should take her out," one of the brothers suggested. I agreed, as did others.

Two weeks later Cindy was killed in a car accident. To this day, no one really knows what happened. The newspaper reported that Cindy had lost control of her car on a rainy night. Her vehicle hydroplaned, went over a bridge, and crashed. I often wondered if that was the real story. Rumors circulated that Wilkinson got tired of being blackmailed and that he had her killed.

It later came to light that Bill Wilkinson was an FBI informant. Bill had been supplying the FBI with names, dates, and places of Klan activities, as well as furnishing the agency with membership applications of everyone who had joined the Klan. When it was discovered, Wilkinson admitted to it. "I just wanted to show the FBI that we had nothing to hide and that we were not an illegal organization," he said.

When they discovered that Bill had given information to the FBI, Klan members were incensed. With threats on his life, Wilkinson dropped out of sight and resigned as imperial wizard. His Klan organization fell apart and "The Invisible Empire" all but ceased to exist. Disgusted with the Klan, I began to party and drink quite a bit.

I didn't really care how reckless I acted during these drinking days. One night a bunch of the boys decided to harass the blacks in their section of Oklahoma City, Oklahoma. This time my brother Terry Don decided to come along.

We drove to a black bar, parked around back, and climbed onto the club's roof. We dropped several big rocks through the skylight that overlooked the dance floor. Many blacks got hit by either glass or rocks that came crashing through the skylight.

We jumped off the roof and ran to the car. As we were driving away, the people who had been in the club were chasing our car. We just sped away.

Then we turned onto another street where hotels for hookers were situated. We drove up to the front of a room where we had seen two hookers, one black and one white, looking out the window at us.

One of the boys with us, Kevin (who happened to be an Oklahoma policeman's son), went to their room. They told him that they wanted $25 a piece. Kevin told them he just wanted to watch television. They told him to either give them the money or leave. He came back to the car, and my brother Terry Don went into their room. They told him they needed $25.

"There ain't no way I'm going to pay that," he told them. "Besides, I heard that you Negro girls give it away for free."

They started demanding that he leave. One of the girls went over to the blinds and started opening and closing them, signaling their pimp for help. As soon as Terry Don got back into the car, we drove off before their pimp arrived.

The night was young, and we still had lots of energy left. We drove to Will Rogers Park and were looking around when we spotted a homosexual sitting in his car. We decided to beat him up and take his money. The park was notorious as a hangout for gay people — the one group we hated more than blacks. We could tell just by looking at this man that he was as queer as a three dollar bill. As we pulled alongside him, one of the guys in our car started talking to him as if he were gay too. He invited the homosexual to a party and asked him if he would like to follow our car. He said yes.

We could not decide where we wanted to lead him, but we finally pulled over in a dark residential area. We stopped in front of a house, and I got out of the car with two other guys. We started walking toward the house to make him think we were going inside. Terry Don walked over to the man's car and had planned to hit him as he was getting out.

But as soon as Terry Don drew back his fist, he screamed in surprise, "The queer has a gun." Just then Kevin pulled out a 12 gauge shotgun from our car and started shooting at the man's car as he sped away. We jumped back into our car and started chasing him up and down the streets of Oklahoma City. Sometimes we hit speeds of 80 or 90 miles per hour on residential streets.

We continued to shoot, but we never hit him. We lost him on one of those residential streets. We were fighting mad and wanted to teach someone a lesson, so we decided to go back to find the hookers and their pimps.

We pulled alongside a young, black teenage hooker as she walked down the street. After learning she charged $25, Terry Don agreed and motioned for her to climb into the car. She looked inside, saw five white boys, and said, "No way. I'm not going to get into this car." We tried to convince her that we were on the up and up. After a few minutes, she said, "Okay, pull up to the corner under the street lamp."

We pulled forward, and just as she approached the back of the car, Kevin opened the front passenger door, climbed out, pointed his shotgun at her, and said, "Get in, nigger." The poor girl started screaming and running down the street. We all laughed, and Kevin got back into the car.

Suddenly, a shot rang out. Behind us were two carloads of pimps shooting at us. We sped away as fast as we could and drove onto the freeway via the exit ramp. A truck was heading toward us. At the last minute, we swerved to get out of its way and did a U-turn on the freeway.

"Well, boys, I think we should call it a night and head home!" I sighed with relief.

No one disagreed with me.

On one of my drinking binges, I met a young girl named Londa. I fell in what I thought was love.

Londa and I went out a couple of times. Then I found out she was hanging around punk rockers and homosexuals. Londa never knew about my Klan activities. We broke up because of her involvement with homosexuals, which was totally against my beliefs. I wanted to get back at her friends because I felt that they were the reason for us splitting up.

Deciding to crash a big party planned by some homosexuals, I called my Klan brethren and told them to put on their hoods and prepare some Molotov cocktails. We learned this party would be held in a public park in the middle of the night. I figured there would be about 30 of them present.

What was my strategy? We would throw some Molotov cocktails at their cars and shoot up the park. Then we would tell them to disband their little groups or we would come back to get them. I was doing this to convince the Klan that we needed to get those homosexuals, but for the most part I just wanted to scare Londa into coming back to me. I didn't tell the klansmen that, though.

It was a nice crisp night, just the right setting for kluxing. As we drove there in silence, I felt the excitement buzzing in the car. We pulled up and all five of us got out, wearing our sheets and hoods.

We each lit one of the Molotov cocktails and threw them down the hill. There was a big explosion and the area burst into flames. About 250 homosexuals and punk rockers started screaming and running. Some of them spotted us in our sheets at the top of the hill, and they ran toward us throwing rocks and bottles.

The plan fell apart, and we panicked and pointed guns at them. They froze for a second, then one of the guys with me who had a shotgun said, "Oh no, the gun is jammed!" I fired a pistol point blank into the crowd. Surprisingly, no one was hit.

We jumped in the car and took off. While carloads of party goers were following and throwing debris at us, I was leaning out the window shooting at them. Because my hood obstructed my view, I removed it, which led to my being identified.

One of the cars rammed the back of our car as we were speeding down the freeway. Our driver lost control and our car hydroplaned past an exit ramp and crashed into a fence outside of a McDonald's fast food restaurant. We jumped out of the car just before it caught fire and burst into flames.

Amazingly, not one of us was hurt. We stopped long enough to see that everyone was intact, and then we fled behind the McDonald's and into a little creek. Someone had called the police, and they were all over the place looking for us.

The police found our car and wasted no time tracing the license plate. They discovered to whom the car was registered and contacted his parents. We did not know it at the time, but his parents were headed toward our location.

Somehow in the excitement our group got split up. We were running in all directions. The police took advantage of the confusion and ultimately caught everyone except me.

One of the guys confessed and told the police everything, including that it was all my plan. The police caught up with me. I did not have to go to jail, however, because the father of one of the klansmen was one of the arresting officers.

The police knew if they pressed charges against me, they had to charge the officer's son too, so they made a deal with the party goers. If we paid for their car, the homosexuals wouldn't press charges. That's exactly what happened. Charges were never filed. I never paid for the damages either.

I was pretty upset by that whole situation, and I began to drink heavily again. I was disgusted that nothing seemed to work out for me. I called Londa, wanting to get back together with her, but she refused. She wanted to start going to church and suggested that I do the same. Maybe she was right. I needed a change.

I attended Crossroads Cathedral in Oklahoma City for a while and thought I had found some peace for my life. The congregation didn't treat me as I had expected. These warm and caring people didn't know about my past. Once they found out, I figured things would change. But it didn't.

Dan Sheaffer, the pastor, often talked about blacks in the Bible, a subject that truly fascinated me. I became very involved with the church and even tried to give my life to God. I attended classes and became a regular member. But I refused to renounce my allegiance to the Klan, and pretty soon the two began to clash. One of them would have to go. After six months of faithful attendance, I quit the church without so much as a goodbye to anyone.

I got involved with professional wrestling for a while, and even became Arkansas Heavyweight Champion. I retained the title until 1988 and retired as champion. I quit because a lot of wrestling promoters banned me when they found out I was involved with Tom Metzger and the White Aryan Resistance.

Feeling lonely and wanting some companionship, I began looking for a wife. Sally and I started dating, but I did not tell her about my involvement in white supremacy. We went fishing together, and we went out to the clubs. We did lots of things together, but we never discussed racism or politics. We had a pretty quick courtship, and I eventually asked her to marry me. She was everything I thought I wanted and needed, but I had no business marrying her because I really did not love her.

Even after our marriage I didn't share with her my dark, deep-seated attitudes of hatred, bigotry, and racism and my involvement with the Klan. One day, however, she confronted me about my past. She didn't understand it and, quite frankly, it scared her.

"Why didn't you tell me this before we got married?" she demanded, hurt that I had kept that part of my life hidden from her.

"The issue never came up while we were dating," I replied. "Besides, I've been inactive for some time so I didn't think it really mattered."

# Chapter Fifteen

# White Revolution — the Only Solution!

Even though my wife was apprehensive about my work in the Klan, I maintained an interest in working more closely with Tom Metzger. The Klan and other white supremacist groups, such as Christian Identity and the Skinheads, were starting to rebuild in Tulsa, Oklahoma. Tom Metzger had dropped the name of the California Knights of the Ku Klux Klan, changing it to White American Resistance, and later changing it to White American Political Association (WAPA). Finally it became White Aryan Resistance, or WAR.

Metzger asked me if I would become an organizer for the area. I jumped at the opportunity. This was great. The more we talked about improving the Klan, the more excited I became. I asked him if he would like to visit Tulsa, and he agreed. Metzger said he wanted to schedule a press conference. I called the media and told them that Metzger would be coming to town.

On the day of his arrival I drove to the airport to meet him. Not realizing Metzger's influence and impact, I was in for a real surprise. The media turnout at the airport overwhelmed me. TV crews and journalists had come from all over to cover his visit.

When Metzger stepped off the airplane he had a couple of bodyguards with him. I approached him and shook his hand, informing him that we were going to conduct the conference in the airport. The media immediately began to fire questions at him.

Metzger responded in a cool and calm manner. After the meeting we went back to his hotel to discuss strategies of rebuilding the Klan and organizing WAR in the heartland area. We concluded that "white revolution is the only solution!"

As my friendship with Metzger grew, however, my marriage deteriorated. I did not realize it at the time, but Sally was becoming distant and withdrawn.

My wife was expecting our first child in 1988, and I attributed her moodiness and discontent to the pregnancy. I soon found out otherwise. When I returned one evening after attending a big Klan rally that had been broadcast on television, Sally met me at the door in tears.

"Johnny Lee, I saw you on television with the Klan," she fumed. "I also got several bomb threats while you were gone. If your racist activities are going to jeopardize me or the baby, I'm not going to tolerate them any longer!"

I tried to reason with her, but her family was there and their presence had clearly built a wall between the two of us. Sally decided to leave me, but I managed to talk her into staying until the baby was born. It was due any day.

Unfortunately, I was allowed to see my baby daughter only twice. Because I helped with the delivery, I saw her at birth. I convinced my wife to let me see her a second time on one particular occasion. I have not seen or heard from her since.

My relationship with Metzger was almost like a dream. We went on talk shows together and to many Klan meetings. I learned a great deal about his version of the Klan. He felt the old way was outdated and it was unnecessary to hide beneath those hoods.

Metzger opened a lot of doors. We appeared on Oprah Winfrey's talk show, and I was allowed to speak briefly and answer some questions concerning WAR. The crowd hated Tom and me, booing us at every turn. It was exciting, and I was able to meet with the Klan from Chicago.

When I returned home Sally dropped the bomb on me at the front door.

"I'm going to divorce you, Johnny Lee."

I could not believe what I had just heard. She kept her word. Sally left with our daughter. I was alone, a broken man.

All I had left was my Klan family so I decided to throw myself into my work. I began to recruit very heavily. We tried to find a radio station that would give us air time. This was not an easy task, since no one in this area wanted to be associated with the Klan. We searched throughout Oklahoma before finding a radio station in Claremore that was willing to sell us radio time.

Joe Grego, one of my right hand men, left announcements on his answering machine (which he refers to as his "white power message machine") saying, "The white supremacists now have their own radio show that can be heard every Sunday morning in green country." The next thing I knew it was all over the news: "White supremacists buy radio time!"

The Jewish Federation of Tulsa, the "Just Say No To Hate" committee, and the Racism Task Force, which had formed in Tulsa to combat Klan activities, visited the owner of the radio station. They threatened to go to the Chamber of Commerce and to boycott his station if he didn't cancel us.

Despite their urgings, we were allowed to continue our broadcast. The station owner told them that he promised us four weeks. After the four weeks were completed, he would take us off the air. He later gave us only three weeks to broadcast our program instead of the four that he had promised.

When only two weeks remained on our agreement, the media came to the station and camped outside. Reporters and their camera crews filmed us as we were going in and out of the radio station. We took calls from people inquiring about the activities, operations, and beliefs of the Klan. It caused quite a stir. The owner of the radio station lost a lot of clients who advertised, and he eventually had to sell his radio station because he had sold air time to white supremacists.

Because of this incident and my divorce case, I questioned my ability to be an effective leader. I had retained an attorney to handle my divorce, and the case dragged on. I had heard nothing for a while. A few months later, after I had moved to Tulsa, I called my attorney. When he told me the divorce proceedings were already over, I was stunned.

"What do you mean, I'm already divorced? I was never served with papers, and I never went to a trial."

"A process server testified that he had already served you with the divorce papers and you refused to take them. Therefore, the judge granted the divorce and gave Sally everything," the attorney informed me.

My wife got everything, including custody of our daughter. Every time that I attempted to visit my baby girl, Sally vehemently refused to let me see my child. I told her if I could not see my child, she was not going to get any child support from me.

I tried several times to see my daughter but every time I went she had the sheriff, along with her family, waiting for me. I had to fight her whole family and the sheriff's department just because I was attempting to visit my baby girl. It was always just one big hassle, so I stayed in Tulsa.

I met a woman named Sue Ellen not long after this ordeal, and a few weeks later we decided to get married. My ex-wife Sally contacted me just a few days before the wedding and told me that I had three choices to make. I could either pay $3,000 in back child support, which I did not have, or I could go to jail. In Oklahoma fathers who don't pay child support go to jail.

I thought that I had a right to deny child support since she had denied me the right to see my baby. But the State of Oklahoma almost always sides with the mother, and the father cannot violate the court order to pay under any circumstances — even in a case such as this where Sally refused to allow me to see my daughter.

What was my final choice? Sally gave me the option of signing away my parental rights forever. I was devastated to say the least. Sue Ellen refused to marry me if I had to pay all that back child support. I had spent all my money preparing a home for Sue Ellen and me. I knew no one from whom I could borrow that kind of money. Even my attorney refused to handle this case because I could not pay him.

I reluctantly signed away my parental rights to Savannah Cherie, my daughter, instead of going to jail. I believe someday Savannah will be curious about her real father and will either look for me or read this book. If that is the case, I want her to know the real reason behind my signing away my rights.

Sue Ellen and I did get married, but we did not stay married long. Eight weeks to be exact.

My luck was going from bad to worse, but I couldn't imagine life getting much more disastrous. Soon I met a beautiful woman who said all the right things and pushed all the right buttons. She said that she hated blacks and other minorities. I fell for it hook, line, and sinker. One would think that after the episode with Cindy, I would have learned to be more discerning. But again, I fell in what I thought was love.

We went out on a few dates, and I introduced her to my Klan brothers. They wanted nothing to do with her because they didn't trust her. I found out later that they had very good reason for not doing so. She was gathering information and names to give to the police. She had succeeded in getting several names before she was found out.

Needless to say, this brought me a few more problems that I didn't need. My right hand man, who was gunning for my position, wanted to see me mess up and this was the one thing he thought he could use. First, he rallied the men against me, and then he decided to tell Metzger that I had jeopardized the Klan by allowing this woman to come in and infiltrate the organization. They told Metzger that I was no longer loyal to WAR.

Grego had succeeded in taking my old position by becoming Metzger's right hand man. I felt like I had been knifed in the back, but I was determined to succeed. The anger toward Joe did not last long. We decided to patch things up and try to work together for the betterment of the white race.

Meanwhile Metzger's WAR had vowed to work with the Klan as well as other white supremacist groups to overthrow the federal government. Publicly Metzger told the KKK he would work with them, but in private (usually while sipping on a glass of bourbon and smoking a cigar) Metzger called the Klan, Ku Klux Klowns. He had said that the Klan was dead.

Metzger also bragged to me that he no longer believed in the Bible, calling it an "old science fiction book." He declared himself an atheist. For a while, he claimed to believe in the gods of Apollo, Thor, and Isis.

Metzger appointed a boy named Bob Heick to take over as president of the Skinheads in WAR, which he called The American Front. Bob Heick was dating Lavena LeVay, the daughter of Anton LeVay, founder of the Church of Satan in San Francisco, and author of the satanic bible. I did not know about this until right before I had a fallout with Metzger.

Some of the skinheads from Tulsa went to visit Heick in San Francisco. They returned to Tulsa telling me about meeting Anton LeVay and seeing satanic pentagrams and skull heads with black candles in Bob's headquarters. When I later confronted Metzger about this, he told me, "Knock off the crap, and come down to earth. You need to accept the fact that WAR works with anybody who will promote the white race, whether they are atheists, satanists, or Christians."

Tom and I eventually parted company in 1989. Our views were no longer the same. He was willing to associate with anyone no matter who they were.

Metzger later began to work with a group called Church of the Creator, which promotes a book called *The White Man's Bible.* This book denounces Christianity and calls Jesus a "Jew on a Stick." Metzger laughed about this and called Jesus that himself. He also told me that he hated the apostle Paul, calling him a murdering Jew bastard. Metzger even bragged to me that he once went to a pagan festival and put on fur chaps and danced around the fire.

Metzger sacrificed his wife and children to promote his ideas of hatred. One must be taught to hate like my father taught me. John Metzger, Tom's son, is a chip off the old block. John learned hate from his father. Today, John is probably even more hateful than Tom.

On TV talk shows, John Metzger comes across to the audience as polite and intelligent, but when he gets on his soap box of hate he resorts to name calling when he feels he is losing ground. Tom and John Metzger's eyes are blinded by hate, the same hate that blinded my eyes also.

After the split between Tom and me, the grand dragons of the Ku Klux Klan approached me and asked me to become their imperial wizard. At 30 years old, I accepted their invitation. Finally, after all these years, I became top man in the Ku Klux Klan. I thought it would bring me fulfillment.

When David Duke sent that man to see me when I was 14 years old, he told me that I would be a future leader in the Klan. What he spoke finally came true. I had arrived. I managed to build up the base of the Klan. The organization had grown and gained momentum. We came up with an idea that would help to bring all the Klans together.

Getting the various splinter groups of the KKK to cooperate with each other in a more united front was and still is the greatest of challenges. Letters were sent out to different Klan units all across the country.

Richard Butler and the Aryan Nations compound was having a march to commemorate the Sam Davis memorial in Pulaski, Tennessee, where the Klan was formed on Christmas Eve 1865. Sam Davis, a confederate soldier, went to his death in an attempt to fight for the white race and the allegiance of the South. He was hung by the Northern abolitionists and the Yankee Army. Instead of revealing where his confederate comrades were, he chose to die at the hands of his captors. The Klan made a hero out of this man; he was a martyr to them.

White supremacist groups from all over the country came to march and participate in the Sam Davis parade. Several Klan leaders responded to our letters, saying that if the Klan did unite as one Klan, they would support it.

# Chapter Sixteen

## Scared Straight

Finally, after all the planning and the preliminaries had been carried out, many Klan members from my regent came together to ride down to this great meeting. There were several carloads going; a couple of skinheads went in the car with me.

Dennis Mahon, a klansman, took another carload of people. He was quite a character. As large as the Klan was in Kansas City, with several hundred members who were all registered to vote, he ran for city council and received only a few votes. Yet, he claimed to be the big leader of the Klan in his city.

It was rumored that Dennis met a Jewish girl in a bar and didn't know she was Jewish. He promised her that she could be head of the women's auxiliary of the Klan. He moved into her apartment the next day. After she called her father to tell him the exciting news, her father showed up with her brothers and evicted Dennis.

The father turned to his daughter and said, "You are not joining the Klan. You are Jewish."

"She didn't tell me she was Jewish," Dennis allegedly replied.

"With a name like Goldstein, you didn't know she was Jewish?" the father supposedly asked in amazement.

Because of incidents like this, Dennis was considered a laughingstock among the Klan.

As we drove to Pulaski, the skinheads got excited and pretty rowdy. We decided to stop in Nashville, Tennessee to eat pizza. The skinheads got obnoxious in the restaurant and talked about blowing people away. I guess somebody panicked and called the police. We definitely did not want to disrupt all our planning and hard work by ending up in jail. We packed everyone back in the cars and headed down the highway.

Not long after we were on the road again, I saw a sign for Pulaski. Realizing something was wrong, I pulled off thinking that I might have passed the correct sign. I drove into a gas station and asked for directions. A guy standing there routed us 35 miles out of the way into Lewisberg, where the Tennessee

State Patrol had set up a roadblock for us. Several vehicles barricaded the exit, and the troopers were outside their cars with their guns drawn.

After instructing us to get out of the vans, the officers beat us and handcuffed us. I kept asking, "What did we do?" I knew we had rights, but they didn't want to hear anything we had to say. They searched our vans, tearing up the inside. Finding some unloaded guns in the van, one of the officers said, "They aren't loaded." Another officer replied, "Find their bullets and load them." Then they said we had violated a weapons law.

They took us to the police station, but they never read us our rights. Confining our group to a cell, they called us out one by one. They asked each of us why we had guns. When it was my turn, I said we just brought the guns down to do a little target practice and they were unloaded.

They refused to believe us. Thinking we were going to start trouble, they decided to keep us in jail. We protested their reluctance to give us our standard phone calls. I found out later that they put us under strict orders, and we were not allowed to have phone calls.

I remembered what had happened in Mississippi in 1964 to three civil rights workers. They were arrested by the local Mississippi law enforcement, Deputy Sheriff Cecil Ray Price. The civil rights workers were held in jail and were not given phone calls either. They were released at midnight and, unbeknownst to them, the Klan was waiting for them.

They killed them and buried them in a dam in Mississippi. Ironically, that crime was perpetrated by the Klan and here were klansmen about to be the victims of the same crimes that our organizations were guilty of committing years earlier.

Just thinking about that gave me the chills. What if they wanted to do that with us? No one knew where we were, and no one would ever find us. I was on the verge of panic.

Time seemed to stand still while we sat in that jail cell. We still had not been booked, but I received a ray of hope when one of the jailers asked to shake my hand. *Oh no,* I thought, *he's going to kick me between the legs.* Reluctantly, I extended my hand and he gave me the secret Klan handshake.

This Klan brother allowed me to use the phone when everyone else left. I called Tom Metzger, and he immediately contacted a white supremacist attorney from Texas. The attorney was in Tennessee to attend the march, and he immediately went to work on our behalf. The next morning attorney Kirk Lyons was there to post our bail. He transported us directly to the march. The police were surprised to see us there. We just saluted them and walked by.

After the march I spent most of the afternoon with attorney Lyons getting my van and other property out of impoundment. When I finally arrived back at the meeting site, I learned that all kinds of fights and arguments had broken out among the rival white supremacist leaders. Months and months of trying to bring all the leaders together in unity had failed.

Different white supremacist leaders had come face to face for the first time in a long while. They had started name calling and accusing each other of stealing each other's mailing lists, members, and other things. Two white supremacist leaders started fighting and chasing each other around the table. I had to step in and grab them. Pete Peters, a Christian Identity white supremacist preacher, was booed, jeered, and attacked by skinheads. Some klansmen started beating up skinheads and visa versa.

The people who allowed us to use their property were so mad that they asked several people to leave. This totally disgusted me. Is this what I had spent 17 years of my life in the Klan for? We talk about unity for the white race, but disunity flourishes among us. So much hate fills our organizations that it spills over on each other. We cannot get along with one another when our different groups come together.

After the fiasco in Pulaski, Tennessee, I decided to get out of the Klan. We headed back to Oklahoma. This whole incident left me shaken and angry, but I wanted to put it behind me. Since it had happened in a different state, I figured that no one would know about it. I was wrong. The incident made the front page of our local newspaper. I lost my job because my employer found out I was part of the Klan. Unfortunately, this wasn't new. I had lost many jobs because of my white supremist views.

The Mahon brothers, who were second in command to me, had met a girl by the name of Laurali while in Tennessee and had moved her back to Oklahoma with them. The girl, a professed atheist and a bisexual, had had numerous lesbian affairs.

That did it for me. I wanted out of the Klan for good. Six months after being named imperial wizard, I turned over the "keys to the kingdom" to Dennis Mahon, telling him he could have it for good.

The next year was a blur. I slipped into a depression that I just couldn't shake. Nothing seemed to matter to me anymore. Reflecting on my life, I felt I had nothing to live for. No family, no wife, no job. Feeling worthless, I thought I would never amount to anything.

Wanting to end my life, I decided to commit suicide. Before I could pull the trigger, however, I remembered that the only truly happy experiences in my life occurred while I attended church as a child. *Maybe I need to go back to church,* I thought to myself. I felt like the prodigal son. I longed to return to God, my Creator and Father.

First, however, I needed to completely disengage myself from the Klan. The only way I could get out with my life was to make them think I was a drunk with no concern for anything but the bottle. It took some time, but my plan worked. Eventually, the Klan believed I didn't care for the organization any longer.

# Chapter Seventeen

## The Prodigal Son

After leaving the Klan, I began to read and study the Bible. I had many questions that needed to be answered. Did God actually care for me? After all I had done, could God save me? I knew I had walked away from Him. Would God accept me back?

I had been so evil. As one of the most hateful men in America, I had organized white supremacy groups, harassed blacks and others, and spread my ideas wherever I went. Could God ever forgive me?

One of the first places that the Word of God became real to me was in the Parable of the Prodigal Son. The story describes a father and his two sons. The older son faithfully served him. The younger son, however, asked for his share of the inheritance. The father divided the estate between them.

Not many days later, the younger son went to a distant land and spent his share of the inheritance on wild living. After his money ran out, a severe famine struck the land. Being in need, he hired himself out to a citizen of that country, who sent him into his fields to feed swine. The prodigal longed to fill his stomach with the food that the pigs were eating, but no one gave him anything.

When he came to his senses, the son said, "What am I doing here? Even my father's servants eat better than this. I'll go back and humble myself. I'll ask my father to forgive me and let me be like one of his hired men."

The prodigal began his long journey back home. Ragged, dirty, and hungry, he was a much different sight than the proud young man who had left.

How many times had the father looked down that road, praying his son would return? One day his prayer was answered. Down the road came that ragged, dirty, long lost son. The father dropped everything and rushed to meet the boy. Throwing his arms around the son, he kissed him.

"Father, I've sinned against heaven and against you," the prodigal began. "I'm no longer worthy to be called your son."

Before he could finish his apology, the father spoke to his servants, "Quick! Bring the best robe and put it on him. Put a ring on his finger and sandals on his feet. Bring the fattened calf and kill it. Let's have a feast and celebrate. For this son of mine was dead and is alive again; he was lost and is found" (Luke 15:22-24).

The older son who had stayed by his father's side resented all the fuss over his younger brother. He said to his father, "Look! All these years I've been slaving for you and never disobeyed your orders. Yet you never gave me even a young goat so I could celebrate with my friends. But when this son of yours who has squandered your property with prostitutes comes home, you kill the fattened calf for him!" (Luke 15:29,30).

"My son," the father said, "you are always with me, and everything I have is yours. But we had to celebrate and be glad, because this brother of yours was dead and is alive again; he was lost and is found" (Luke 15:31,32).

Like the lost son, I headed home. My heavenly Father had waited patiently to extend His forgiveness, compassion, and healing to my broken, sinful life.

# Chapter Eighteen

## Renewing the Mind

To this day I don't believe that it was a coincidence. As I picked up my Bible one day, it fell open to a particular passage. I was astounded by what I read:

> There is neither Jew nor Greek, slave nor free, male nor female, for you are all one in Christ Jesus. If you belong to Christ, then you are Abraham's seed, and heirs according to the promise (Galatians 3:28,29).

Then I turned to Acts 17:26 and discovered, "From one man he [God] made every nation of men, that they should inhabit the whole earth . . ."

I couldn't believe these verses were in the Bible. Other than John 3:16, the first verse I had learned as a child, I wasn't very familiar with the Scriptures. For many years, I quoted Jesus' words to the Jews:

> Ye are of your father the devil, and the lusts of your father ye will do. He was a murderer from the beginning, and abode not in the truth, because there is no truth in him. When he speaketh a lie, he speaketh of his own: for he is a liar and the father of it.... He that is of God heareth God's words: ye therefore hear them not, because ye are not of God" (John 8:44,47, KJV).

David Duke taught me that Jesus spoke those words against the Jews. I never read the whole chapter or realized that Jesus was a Jew Himself. I never knew that Jesus directed these words to hypocrites, Pharisees, and those who would not do God's will. David Duke twisted it around and made me think that Jesus told the Jews that they were all children of the devil.

My Klan background gave me a lot of misconceptions about the Bible. I never believed the story about Adam and Eve, specifically the part about Eve eating the apple. We were taught the serpent seed theory, meaning that Eve did not eat an apple. Instead she had sex with Satan, who planted the seed of Cain in her, and then she had sex with Adam, who planted the seed of Abel in her. We were taught that Eve gave birth to half-brother twins. Cain was Satan's son and Abel was Adam's son. That was why God accepted only Abel's offering and not Cain's.

The Klan and Christian Identity taught us that Cain killed Abel out of jealousy and because of the verse that says, "Ye are of your father the devil.... He was a murderer from the beginning . . ." (John 8:44, KJV). They taught that the mark of Cain was the mark of the devil, and Cain had been banished to the land of Nod (meaning the land of darkness), where he married Negro wives and fathered the Jewish race.

The Klan and other Identity Groups and Aryan Nations teach this farfetched theory today. They say the Greek or Hebrew version of the Bible supports this, but most of them have never read Greek or Hebrew. Until I read Scripture for myself, I only believed what I had been told.

During my many years in the Klan, God kept me safe in the hollow of His hand. On countless occasions I escaped serious injury, car accidents, and an untimely death. I'm grateful God didn't give up on me during my rebellion from Him.

Understanding that the Bible had been distorted when it was presented to me, I began to see Scripture in a new light. All the verses I used to quote were taken out of context in the Klan literature that supported our racist views. As a klansman I had carried a Bible around to occasionally look up a verse that appeared in Klan literature, but I didn't know the God who had penned the Scriptures.

Realizing I had no relationship with God, I knelt down and cried out for a new life.

"Lord Jesus, I've been so wrong — just like the prodigal son whose father forgave him. Lord, I thought I knew You all these years, but I realize I didn't know You at all. I want to come to You now. Father, I want You to take this hate from me.

"Come into my heart, Lord Jesus, and cleanse me. Make me a new man. I'll dedicate my life to You, Father. If You forgive me, I'll live the rest of my life for You. Help me to see others the way that You see them. Lord, help me to see that all Your children are the same."

Feeling as if a thousand pounds had been lifted from my shoulders, I just began to praise Him. I lifted my hands to heaven and started speaking in another language. I knew what it was, because I had heard about speaking in tongues. God had just given me His Holy Spirit. At that moment an incredible love came into me and flowed out of me.

I began to study the Scriptures to renew my mind, but I also needed the fellowship of other believers. Wanting to hear sound, biblical teaching, I tried desperately to find the right church. After visiting several churches, I grew discouraged. One day I spotted a newspaper ad that said:

Victory Christian Center
A Church for all Races
Reverend Billy Joe and Sharon Daugherty

I began to attend Victory Christian Center and study God's Word under Pastor Daugherty's ministry. As he shared the truth of God's Word, I took notes. Finally, I was happy to be serving God. My mind was starting to be renewed.

I began to gain respect for others and to meet people of other races. God was transforming me a little at a time. Many burdens that I had carried for years began to disappear. God replaced them with new, wonderful things.

The Bible says, "He who began a good work in you will carry it on to completion until the day of Christ Jesus" (Philippians 1:6). I stood firmly on that promise as my life gradually changed.

# Chapter Nineteen

## Just One

In 1991, I sat in a Sunday morning service at the Oral Roberts University Mabee Center in Tulsa, Oklahoma. During Pastor Billy Joe Daugherty's sermon, the lights went out. When the lights came back on, hundreds of yellow paper starfish rested on the stage. Billy Joe Daugherty, standing next to the starfish, said:

> Picture these starfish washed upon the beach by a heavy tide. Picture a little boy walking along and seeing these thousands of starfish. The little boy said, "Oh my, they're going to die. They've been washed upon the beach." For more than an hour, he frantically picked them up and threw them back into the water.

Soon an older man came along, stepping on the starfish. He walked up to the little boy and said, "Son, may I ask what you're doing?"

The boy said, "I've got to get these starfish back into the water. A big tide washed them onto the beach, and they're going to die if they don't get back into the water. Please, sir, won't you help me?"

The old man said, "Son, you're a fool! I've walked along for over two miles this morning and there are starfish washed up all along the beach. You'll never get them all back into the water. It is impossible. They are all going to die. So you see, son, it really doesn't matter."

The little boy looked down at the starfish. Then he looked up at the old man. He bent down, picked up one of the starfish, and said, "Well, it matters to this one." And he threw that starfish back into the water.

At that moment tears cascaded down my cheeks. The Holy Spirit seemed to nudge me and say, "You know what you've got to do." I jumped out of my seat, went forward in response to the minister's invitation, and surrendered to the call to preach.

"God, if I can show somebody what I had to go through to finally accept the call on my life, it will be worth it," I prayed. "If I can do anything to get someone delivered from the kind of lifestyle that bound me, then my life has not been in vain. I know what You're calling me to do, and I will do it by

Your grace and power. Father God, now I know You have a purpose for my life."

After God called me to preach His Word, I was praying one day in the Spirit, seeking God's direction. Rev. Watts came to mind. Many people planted seeds in my life and prayed for me to change my ways.

My grandmother, Mamie Carter, constantly prayed for me. Leonard Kimble, at the Church of God in Bell Gardens, California, prayed that I would one day change. Rev. Bill Means and Rev. Marvin Cain both prayed for me and witnessed to me more than once. Elder Charles Barnes and Jerry Woody at Crossroads Cathedral in Oklahoma City also prayed for me.

I was also influenced by a book called *Child of Satan, Child of God,* written by Susan Atkins, former right hand girl to Charles Manson. Thinking it glorified white supremacy, as the Manson Family advocated, I purchased the book. Instead I read how Susan received Jesus Christ as her Lord and Savior, and how she was delivered from the influence of Manson and racism.

Today, Susan and I are close friends. She writes to me quite often, and I visit her when I am in Southern California. Susan is truly a new creation in Christ.

When I joined Higher Dimensions Church in Tulsa, Oklahoma, I got to know Pastor Carlton Pearson personally. I found out that he had prayed for me while watching one of my TV appearances on "The Morton Downey Jr. Show" in 1988. I advocated white supremacy on the program.

The person most responsible for planting the seed that eventually changed my life was none other than Rev. Wade Watts. After my conversion to Christ, I called Rev. Watts late one fall day in 1991. I had found his phone number through directory assistance.

His wife answered and called him to the phone, saying, "Wade, this sounds like that old klansman who used to call here years ago!"

Rev. Watts came to the phone and said, "Hello."

I responded, "Hello, brother!"

This pleasantly surprised him. I had called him many things over the years, but I had never called him brother!

"Do you remember John Clary?" I asked.

"I've been praying for you for years!" he responded.

"I left the Klan in 1989. Not only has God saved me, He's called me to preach His Word," I beamed.

"Have you had an opportunity to preach anywhere?"

"Not yet."

"Would you speak in my church?" Rev. Watts asked without hesitation. "I would be honored to host you."

His invitation enabled me to speak at his all-black church, the same church that my fellow klansmen and I had once tried to burn down.

During this time Rev. Watts was pastoring two churches in Oklahoma: one in Muskogee; the other in McAlister. First, I spoke at the church in Muskogee. Eventually I also had an opportunity to address his church in McAlister.

At the church in McAlister I unveiled in great detail the story of my turbulent past. At the end of my testimony, I invited unrepentant sinners to come forward, give their hearts to God, and receive Jesus Christ as their Lord and Savior.

The first person to respond was a young teenage girl. Tears streamed her sweet little face as she said, "I want to ask Jesus into my heart!"

At that moment I heard someone else weeping.

As I turned around I realized, to my amazement, that it was Rev. Watts. Through tears of joy, he said, "John, this is my baby. That same little girl that I showed you when we debated at the radio station back in 1979!"

I couldn't believe it; this was the same baby girl that Rev. Watts had confronted my conscious with over a decade ago. For years his question rang in my mind: "How could you hate this baby, this sweet little baby?"

I had dreamed about that girl for many years, asking myself how could I possibly hate her and other little children like her.

Tia, now a teenager, was a bi-racial child, born to a black father and a white mother. Unwanted by her biological parents, Tia was placed for adoption. Rev. Watts adopted and raised her as his own.

Truly, God is a Father to the fatherless and does indeed provide a home for the orphan. God is a good God, and He's good all the time. God turns stumbling blocks into stepping stones to our glorious future.

When Rev. Watts saw Tia as a baby, he did not consider whether she was black, white, or brown. Rev. Watts saw a baby who needed love, and he chose to love her by adopting and caring for her.

Tia shared with me later that white children referred to her as black, and black children referred to her as white. She had a sincere desire to belong, but she was never accepted exclusively for the wonderful person that she is.

At the time she came to the altar, she wasn't doing well in school and felt miserable deep inside. Tia came to the meeting that night out of curiosity to hear the former imperial wizard of the Ku Klux Klan. She had heard about the incident at the radio station years earlier when Rev. Watts showed her to me.

Twelve and a half years after I debated with this man about my erroneous belief in the black man's inferiority, I ended up preaching in his church — a church that I attempted to burn down. This young girl heard about the love of God from the wicked imperial wizard she had heard about all her life.

On that day in 1991, Tia Watts' name was written in the Lamb's book of life. Rev. Watts had 13 children, and three more came forward when they saw their sister Tia accept Christ.

Rev. Watts' 38-year-old daughter Calooah came forward to receive Jesus. She told me that when she was a child she needed her daddy, but he was never home. Because he was always off working for the NAACP, she resented the organization. He was either out preaching for a church or fighting the Klan. She felt that all three (the church, NAACP, and the Klan) robbed her of her daddy.

When she saw Tia come forward and when she heard my story, however, she decided to ask Jesus into her heart. She concluded that Jesus needed her daddy more than she did.

If I live to see a million miracles, none could ever top what I saw that day. Rev. Wade Watts and I became best friends after that day. I even call him Uncle Wade sometimes. I have grown to love him and his family, and I consider them family to me. Rev. Watts and I have preached services together, and have appeared together on television talk shows hosted by Phil Donahue and Geraldo.

Once I asked Rev. Watts, "Of all the things I did to you, didn't you ever just once want to hate me"?

"Johnny Lee, my daddy once told me, 'Son, when a man hates you, he is sick. You wouldn't want to hate a sick man, would you? You would want to help him get better.' Johnny Lee, when I met you, I knew you were a young man who had been misguided and misled. I wanted to help you get well and healed of the sickness called hate."

Rev. Watts helped me to get healed of hatred by showing me love and by praying for me. I believe that if I follow Rev. Watts' example, people like Tom Metzger, David Duke, and others can also be healed.

Tom hates me, but I do not hate him. I pray that one day soon he will turn to the Lord like I did and ask for forgiveness. Some people do not believe that this is possible, but if Jesus made the blind to see, the deaf to hear, the crippled to walk, and could raise the dead, then He certainly can heal a man from hate and racism.

By the way, Tia Watts graduated from McAlister High School as class valedictorian in 1994. She wanted to go to college, but Rev. Watts told her that he did not have the money to send her. She said, "That's okay, Daddy. I'll pray and ask God to send the money."

A couple of weeks later, Rev. Watts received a telegram from the NAACP that read something like this: "Because of your faithful lifetime service in the NAACP, we are enclosing a $40,000.00 scholarship for your daughter Tia to go to the college of her choice."

Yes, God still answers prayer! Many more Tias — and Johnny Lee Clarys — still need to be reached. That is my job. As a minister of the Lord, I will spend the rest of my life reaching people and fighting hate so that this will be a better world for all of us.

# Epilogue

Once when I appeared on his television talk show, Phil Donahue said to me, "You know, you are a very unusual dude, Johnny Lee Clary!" He turned to the audience and said, "I think it is only fair to say that most don't do as Johnny Lee Clary did. Most people who once had this hatred, this racism, and even go so far as to join a white supremacist group — it becomes your life, and you don't turn around. Once you've got it, you've got it."

But I said to him, "That's right, Phil, but remember this: Hatred is something that you are taught; it is a learned response. You are not born with hatred. There is hope. If God can save me and change my mind, He can save others and change their minds also."

Many people are dissatisfied with themselves for many reasons. We must give them hope. We must give the downtrodden reason to look to the seed of God inside themselves and find happiness and contentment. We must also give those who have wandered from the straight and narrow path a reason to look in the mirror and want to change.

Why have I revealed my turbulent past in such detail? I want others to read about the change that happened to me, as drastic as it was, and know there is still hope for the wayward soul. Those who are lost, devastated, depressed, oppressed, and without hope can know that no matter what they have done or what they are presently doing, Jesus Christ is the only answer.

They must get to know Jesus. Once you get to know Him intimately, Jesus will change your whole life as He did mine. I hope my story will encourage someone who is mired in the same self-denial, racism, hatred, bigotry, or self-dislike that bound me. I trust you will see a reason — and find the desire — to change also.

In 1989, Tom Metzger lost a court case in Portland, Oregon, in which the jury ruled Metzger must pay $12 million in damages to the family of a black man who was murdered by skinheads who were members of his White Aryan Resistance. Metzger lost his home and his business, and immediately afterward his wife died. Metzger, however, still continues to lead the white supremacist movement in the United States despite having suffered severe setbacks.

In 1981, my sister Sandy remarried and has enjoyed a happy marriage to this day. We were finally able to set aside our differences and reconcile. In 1994, after I appeared on "The 700 Club" with Pat Robertson and shared my testimony, the secretary for the grand dragon of the Texas KKK repented and asked Jesus into her heart. Later that same year, I shared my story in Armaugh, Northern Ireland. After hearing my testimony, many Catholics and Protestants came together and were reconciled after 25 years of fighting.

In 1995, my brother Terry Don received Jesus Christ as his Lord and Savior and now attends church on a regular basis. One week after his conversion, he drove past the federal building in Oklahoma City and was 3/4 mile from it when a bomb exploded, killing 167 people. God truly was watching over him.

Finally, in 1995, I moved my ministry to Bakersfield, California and joined Valley Faith Fellowship, an interracial church that is pastored by Juan Juarez and located in Delano, California.

Since my miraculous conversion, I have appeared on The Sally Jesse Raphael show twice, The Geraldo Show twice, The Montel Williams Show, The Phil Donahue Show, ABC World News Tonight with Peter Jennings, A&E's Biography, The 700 Club, and several times on The TBN Praise The Lord Show hosted by close friends Jeff and Reeni Fenholt, Del and Cindy Way, Carlton Pearson, and Mike Purkey.

I have held Racial Reconciliation services at Calvary Temple Church in Kerrville, Texas with Pastors Del and Cindy Way and Victory Christian Center in Tulsa, Oklahoma with pastors Billy Joe and Sharon

Daugherty. Bishop George McKinney and I spoke for Promise Keepers in Montgomery, Alabama. I also spoke at a Racial Reconciliation service at St. Stephens Church of God in Christ in San Diego, California which Bishop McKinney pastors. I was also featured at Carlton Pearson's Azusa 1993 and 1994 national conferences in Tulsa, Oklahoma. I now travel throughout the world sharing the good news of Jesus Christ.

# APPENDIX I

# WHITE SUPREMACY

## ARYAN NATIONS

### Oath of Allegiance

"I, as a free Aryan man, hereby swear an unrelenting oath upon the green graves of our sires, upon the children in the wombs of our wives, upon the throne of God Almighty, sacred is His name, to join together in holy union with those brothers in this circle and to declare forthright that from this moment on I have no fear of death, no fear of foe; that I have a sacred duty to do whatever necessary *to deliver our people from the Jew* and bring total victory to the Aryan race.

"I, as a Aryan warrior, swear myself to complete secrecy to the Order and total loyalty to my comrades.

"Let me bear witness to you, my brothers, that should one of you fall in battle, I will see to the welfare and well-being of your family.

"Let me bear witness to you, my brothers, that should one of you be taken prisoner, I will do whatever is necessary to regain your freedom.

"Let me bear witness to you, my brothers, that should an enemy agent hurt you, I will chase him to the ends of the earth and remove his head from his body.

"And furthermore, let me bear witness to you, my brothers, that if I break this oath, let me forever be cursed upon the lips of our people as a coward and an oath breaker.

"My brother, let us be His battle ax and weapons of war. Let us go forth by ones and twos, by scores and by legions, and as true Aryan men with pure hearts and strong minds face the enemies of our faith and our race with courage and determination.

*"We hereby invoke the blood covenant and declare that we are in a full state of war and will not lay down our weapons until we have driven the enemy into the sea and reclaimed the land which was promised to our fathers of old, and through our blood and His will, becomes the land of our children to be."*

It is impossible to discuss the aspirations and motivations of the Ku Klux Klan without dedicating a significant amount of the discussion to the origin, formation, and dynamics of the socio-political and racial ideology of white supremacy. The socio-political ideology and racial-religious doctrine of white supremacy combined with fear, personal insecurity, and racial hatred drive the actions of the KKK and all other white supremacist organizations.

When we talk about the socio-political ideology of white supremacy, we refer to a held system of beliefs that are carried out by two distinct group of people, provoked by two distinct motivations. One form of white supremacy is isolated to the beliefs that white people are superior to all other races or ethnic groups and that America is the divinely ordained basin of all accomplished and progressive white citizens of the world.

*Advocates of this particular element of white supremacy believe it is their moral, God-given, and civic right and duty to eradicate any other ethnic group or race that poses a threat to their way of life.*

White supremacists of this caliber feel that the only human way possible for the white population of America to survive and remain autonomous is that they live in total separation from all other races and ethnic groups. Advocates of this particular element of white supremacist thought are extremely fanatical and often terroristic in the implementation of their beliefs.

White supremacists of this sort include the Ku Klux Klan, Tom Metzger's White Aryan Resistance, Richard Butler's Aryan Nation, Skinheads, Neo-Nazis, and many others. These groups are usually motivated by a combination of fear, insecurity, and hatred. *This fear results from having to compete with minorities for jobs, housing, and other commodities, privileges, and rights that they feel should be offered first and exclusively to them as the descendants and inheritors of the so-called founders of this great land.*

*White men who are racist especially feel insecure because they feel forced to accept America's multicultural and multiracial society, which weakens their strength as the nation's historical privileged class.* Hatred of Jews, blacks, and other minorities by these white supremacist groups is the result of their leaders exploiting racial differences of minorities and holding them up as scapegoats for all of America's social and racial problems.

This is clearly depicted in the "Oath of Allegiance" of the Aryan Nations:[1]

## AMERICA'S CULTURAL ICON

The other side of this spectrum is white supremacy that embraces or more accurately is exclusively expressed through the culture of traditional white middle-class America. By exclusively, I mean the expression of a culture that is isolationist and arrogant in the sense that they believe that any and all other cultures in this diverse nation exist for the furtherance of the dominant culture (the white ruling class).

Second, the dominant culture believes that the only way western American culture can survive is if all other existing cultures are required or rather demanded to assimilate into its cultural expression. This is an element of white supremacy because the dominant culture operates under the assumption and conviction that Eurocentric cultural expression is supreme to all others.

The common theme of this element or expression of white supremacy is greed. Those who hold this conviction have purposely and with great intent misread the words of Jesus, "A man's life does not consist in the abundance of his possessions" (Luke 12:15), to mean that the spiritual and moral worth of a man or woman depends upon one's bank account.

This unrestrained greed motivated white Americans to enslave millions of black people for the sole purpose of providing inexpensive labor to work and bring forth the fruit and harvest of this great land we refer to as "the land of the free and the home of the brave." The determining factor for slavery was not race or skin color but economics — greed!

The present and past inhumane and unjust political and governmental policies that are made in this nation have very little to do with racism and everything to do with greed and servitude (idolatry) to the God of mammon. Race has served only as a medium and an issue of emotional manipulation. What is most troubling about this? The church, showing conspicuous neglect in addressing issues of race and economical morality, has allowed this spirit of greed to even infiltrate and dictate in many ways the culture of Christianity.

Until the American church is willing to address the role that political and cultural white supremacy has upon Western Christianity's interpretation and application of Scripture, its cultural expressions, ecclesiastical functions, operations, and decision-making policies, every attempt at racial reconciliation will only be futile and superficial at best.

# APPENDIX II

# THE CHURCH AND AMERICAN RACISM

When attempting to seek viable solutions for America's greatest social disorder — racism — one must consider a number of diverse dynamics that contribute to its function and existence. First, we must understand that racism in this country did not develop in a vacuum. Second, we must understand that racism is not a 20th century phenomenon.

Racism has a long history. Racism in America is as old as America. When we look at the historical formulation of racism in this nation, we discover that almost since the inception of this nation, the church and the Bible have been used to validate governmental and political racism as well the legal sanction for the European slave trade.

The traditional text of Scripture that has been used to validate racism and slavery has been the misinterpretation of Genesis 9:23 and 24. This particular passage speaks of an incident in which Noah, the

Old Testament patriarch, was discovered lying naked in a drunken stupor in his tent by his grandson Canaan. Ham, the youngest son of Noah and the father of Canaan, also viewed Noah in this state and reported the situation to his two older brothers Shem and Japhet (supposedly in a mocking manner).

Upon hearing the news about the state of their father, they entered the tent backwards with a blanket on their back in an attempt to cover their father's nakedness, consequently also covering their father's drunkenness. When Noah awakened the next day and learned what his grandson and younger son had done, he became angry, declaring a curse against Ham's son, Canaan.

Since many theologians and historians have mistakenly concluded that Ham was the father of the black race, many white Christians were led to believe that this curse extended to all people of Negroid features or African descent. Motivated by a white supremacist-oriented society, some white Christians developed an erroneous and unfounded theory that implied the blackness of skin tone in Africans resulted from the curse that Noah imposed upon his grandson Canaan.

Some white clergy and Christians alike used this particular biblical passage, emphasizing the issue of servitude, to validate and sanction slavery, racism, exploitation, oppression, terrorism, and every other cruel and evil deed and inconceivable wicked act against blacks.

Wayne Perryman, author of *The 1993 Trial on the Curse of Ham,* writes this in reference to biblical exploitation for mistreatment against blacks:

> Many Christians used the alleged curse as legal grounds to outlaw marriages between blacks and whites. Others used it to deny blacks the position of priesthood within their denomination, and still others used the curse theory to justify using blacks as slaves.

> Yes, the so called "Curse on Ham" was the inspiration and justification for the mistreatment of blacks in America. The "Curse Theory" inspired new laws limiting a verity of opportunities to blacks and justified city, state, and federal governments to permit separate rest rooms, restaurants, schools, and drinking fountains. There was one set of facilities for black people and another for all others. It inspired new studies and research to see why (*supposedly*) blacks were inferior. It justified insensitive joke telling and other inhumane treatment directed toward blacks. Blacks felt there was no end to their nightmare.

> The sad commentary to all of this was the fact that the "Curse Theory" was started by white Bible-believing Christians, who in turn introduced this theory to the rest of society.

> Even though they had no evidence to support the so called curse, their story (based on circumstantial evidence), was persuasive enough to convince blacks themselves that they were indeed the descendants of a cursed people.[2]

In part and in more ways than one the church has been used as the vehicle to export and exploit racist beliefs, doctrines, and philosophies in America and abroad.

Beliefs are convictions or positions presented on the basis of reason and evidence. People do not adopt beliefs "for no reason" or without cause, but for reasons and with causes presented by their culture....

Racist norms have suited interests, met needs and served purposes in this society. They enable people to "feel good about themselves," and also to justify any other benefits derived from treating other people as inferior....

Only in the weird ideological surrealism of recent experience has it become clear how racism has always been supported by American *religious*, social, economic, and political thought, and even by our formal philosophy.[3]

Since the church has been responsible for the spread of racism toward blacks, it must be held accountable in its responsibility in helping to eradicate racism. This must no longer be done by the silent disapproval of racist actions but by aggressively dispelling racist attitudes and thinking through proclamation of the Word of God — not only in word but also in making restitution for this nation's 400 years of manipulation, exploitation, and terroristic oppression of African Americans.

# APPENDIX III

# THE SOLUTION

Although there have been many political and governmental attempts at reconciling the issue of race and racism in this nation, very little has been done in the way of a spiritual effort rooted in the will and Word of God. Martin Luther King, Jr. said some 30 years ago, "You can legislate behavior, but you cannot legislate morality." And that is exactly the dilemma we find ourselves in at this moment in history.

We have in many instances made great gains in changing the racist behavior of the citizens of this great nation. We have fallen far short, however, on the issue of changing racist attitudes. And it is the racist attitude of Americans, Christians as well as non-Christians, that threatens to tear away the moral fiber and conscious of this nation.

We are, in many significant ways, bent on reliving the injustices, hatreds, bigotry, and struggles of the past. Since the inception of this democracy, racist attitudes and mind-sets have dic'ated a privileged class that is overwhelmingly distinguished by white males and a poverty class that is disproportionately distinguished by blacks and minorities.

As far as the American community is concerned, the African American community and related groups function to support and service its dominance. The white community legislates, enforces, and reinforces the role function and behavioral boundaries of the African American community in accordance with its dominance needs....

As long as African Americans perform according to the roles prescribed for them by the white community ego complex; as long as they maintained their defined places and form the background against which the preferred white American complex is projected; as long as they reasonably fit the self-serving stereotypes imposed on them by the white American complex, the African American community attains a functional invisibility....[4]

We have failed to learn from the mistakes of the past. Politicians are once again using the race card for political leverage. Hate groups — both black and white — are on the rise and their memberships are increasing drastically. Inner city schools have once again become segregated.

In the most racially diverse and multicultural nation on the face of the earth, 11:00 a.m. on Sunday — the nation's recognized worship hour — is still the most segregated hour in American society. We continue to insist, however, that we love God and our country is a Christian nation built on godly and biblical principles.

Many of the principles that were used to govern this democracy in its genesis were and are bibliocentric. The reality of those principles, however, is not the issue at hand. Since the beginning of this nation, the integrity of those principles has fallen short of validity.

Our blatant and continued hypocrisy (I speak specifically in regard to the church) is the problem, especially in regard to the sin of racism. What do we need in this nation? Beginning with the household of God, may He grant us outward, public, heartfelt, complete and sincere repentance.

## FRUITS WORTHY OF REPENTANCE

Repentance doesn't merely mean the verbal and publicly declared confession of the sins of racism, bigotry, and prejudice. Scriptural repentance is characterized by spiritual, moral, and material action. As John the Baptist told the multitude, "Bring forth therefore fruits worthy of repentance" (Luke 3:8, KJV). Our lifestyles must be worthy of (or consistent with) repentance. This repentance must be characterized by proven actions and motivations that cause us once again to trust one another in areas that once divided us by race, color, and even gender.

The moral act of repentance is not, contrary to evangelistic thinking, exclusively the act of confessing our sins to God. Confession of sins to God and man is only the initial step toward fulfilling the godly mandate for all men to repent of sin. Repentance actually constitutes the absolute changing of one's mind in response to a particular trespass against God and mankind. Inevitably that change of mind should have a great bearing upon one's future actions.

## Endnotes

[1] James Ridgeway, Blood in the Face (New York: Thunder's Mouth Press, 1990), p. 89.

[2] Wayne Perryman, The 1993 Trial on the Curse of Ham (Bakersfield, CA: Pneuma Life Publishing, 1994), p. 6,7.

[3] Thomas Powell, The Persistence of Racism In America (Rowman & Littlefield Publishers, Inc. 1993), p. 2,3,6.

[4] Amos N. Wilson, "Black on Black Violence," African World InfoSystems, 1990, p. 6.

## To Buy More Copies of
## Johnny Lee Clary's
## *Boys In the Hoods*
## Contact Your Local Bookstore

*Send all correspondence to:*
*Johnny Lee Clary*
*P.O. Box 6363*
*Bakersfield, CA 93386*